MW01681518

Dream House Debt Free

8–12 years from now

Craig A. Anderson

Overflowing resources

Overflowing Resources Publishing Company

7375 M 140 South

Eau Claire, MI 49111

ISBN-13: 978-1-950012-00-8

United States of America

Overflowing Resources Publishing Company is a subsidiary of Family Focused Financial. famfocfinancial.com

Book cover designed by germancreative, through fiverr.com

Print and eBook layout by bookwrangler, through fiverr.com

Dream House Debt Free / Craig A. Anderson—1st ed.

Contents

CREDITS

Thank you, Timothy Brandt. Your research, vision, and accountability helped get this book rolling.

Thank you, Hannah Lannigan. Your brainstorming led to the first of many additions and reconstructions.

Thank you, Jim Wing. Your ideas helped develop this work thematically.

Thank you, Claudia Zebell. Your intentional treatment not only improved the work, but your encouragement also made me believe this information could help other people.

Thank you, Andrew Fisher. Your meticulous attention to detail cleaned up this story enough for my wife to take it seriously.

Thank you, Jody Anderson, my wife. Your scrutiny helped me scrub enough elements that a publisher could take the story seriously.

Thank you, Jenny Cummings, Janice Guckenberger, Kathleen Bradford, William Muller, Ben Anderson, Micah Anderson, Linda Diltz, and Emily Schatz for your editorial laundering. You each noticed different points that needed deleting, clarifying, formatting, etc.

I admire all of you and appreciate your help deeply.

—Craig A. Anderson

INTRODUCTION

I remember a kid named Tim who bought bulk candy at wholesale prices, sold most of it at retail prices to classmates, and kept some "free" candy to eat. Perhaps you remember someone who was this clever. Such people understand this principle: have things help pay for themselves.

What if we apply this approach to a purchase as large as a house?

Before you convince yourself that this idea is far-fetched, I want to assure you that this book contains a way to help you get there. How do I know? I am a financial planner who has met with hundreds of people over the last 20 years. I have had the privilege of seeing people's financial decisions and consequences in a time-lapsed photographic view. I've seen where financial decisions and habits lead 20 and 30 years later-what works well and what turns out poorly. This book is a boiled-down composite of many of those real-life outcomes presented in a story format for easier digestion.

You might say, "But you don't know my situation. I don't have much money. I have never bought a house, let alone a dream house."

Think about the candy plan above. It required time, work, and some money. But Tim felt it was worth it to get "free" candy. In a similar way, if you want to live in your dream house debt-free in eight to twelve years, you can! It will require time, work, and money, but by following the tips in this guide, you can do it.

Besides, if you follow what I am proposing, there is something much greater at stake than owning a dream house without debt.

Once you pay off the mortgage, if you keep putting the equivalent of your house payments into an investment account each month, the excitement is just beginning. The amount of money you could save for retirement and the number of years you could add to your early retirement is phenomenal. This guidebook illustrates how dramatically the dream house proposition could impact the financial course of your entire life.

For most of us, housing is one of the greatest expenses over our lifetime. If not managed properly, it can cause us to crash financially or at least lag way behind, much like having a flat tire in a race.

On the other hand, if we manage our housing properly, we can really speed ahead financially. This book is about how to save and make hundreds of thousands of dollars while managing our housing arrangements. By applying the ideas in this book, we can make our house pay off—really pay off.

There are two racetracks offered. If you want a more passive approach, you can drive on the fast track by optimizing your money and paying off your house in twelve to fifteen years.

The second track is for those who are willing to also roll up their sleeves. You can use sweat equity to take an even faster approach. By adding some financial accelerators to the fast track ideas, the faster track should get you into your dream house debt-free in eight to twelve years or less.

The goal is not for you to follow every idea in this book, but rather for you to apply the ideas that sound most workable for your own situation. I hope you will be inspired to think creatively about how you can significantly accelerate your progress toward having your dream house debt-free.

My sincere wish is that you gain many practical tips through this guide. If that's all you receive, your investment in buying and reading this book will be repaid many times over. My deeper desire is that this story changes the financial trajectory of your life for the better. The payoff in this case would be very handsome, and I would appreciate hearing your story. My deepest hope is that this is not just a book, or a story, but an experience that helps you become a different person. If so, I would love to meet you. You are the one for whom I ultimately wrote this book.

Disclaimer

There are many numbers presented in this book to illustrate the principles to be applied. The interest rates used are not intended to reflect current rates, as these are always changing. The housing prices start out lower because this story spans several decades. Even then, the housing prices will not be typical for all parts of the country, especially not for higher-priced markets. You'll notice, rather, the real estate prices and interest rates given are conservative figures used simply for example. The higher house prices and/or interest rates are when you read this, the more dramatic your potential savings can be by following these ideas.

Also, most numbers will be rounded off for illustration purposes. They aren't intended to be precise or to provide promises of what will happen in your situation. They are just examples to help you see the power of applying these principles to your life.

Some who read this book will achieve results that far exceed the numbers presented here. For example, my daughter and her husband paid off their first house in three years. Others will have less impressive results. However, I believe everyone who takes this pursuit seriously will make much greater progress toward owning their dream house than he or she would have done without employing these ideas. It is like taking shortcuts.

This book is not intended to provide legal, tax, financial planning, or real estate advice. Please see a trusted local professional for personal recommendations.

—Craig A. Anderson, ChFC®

President, Family Focused Financial

PART 1—GETTING ON THE TRACK

If You Should Buy a House and How to Do So

Meet Sofia

When everyone pulled up to her house for dinner one Friday night, Sofia met them at the curb. They were puzzled. Sofia was a great cook and a fun hostess, so any party at her house would include lots of good food and laughter. Why wasn't she inside finishing up the meal as usual?

> SOFIA: Thank you for coming to my house tonight. But this isn't my house....

Her friends looked at each other completely puzzled. They had been here many times for dinner over the years. They even knew her next door tenant, Rick. What could she possibly mean? This was her address and she was here, so this was obviously the right house.

> SOFIA: Follow me.

She hopped in her car and took off. They followed, wondering if this was a game. After a few minutes, she pulled over and parked. They followed her but didn't know where they were or why Sofia had led them there.

Sofia enjoyed their quizzical looks and thought back to what had happened the day before.

The Day Before

It had been the culmination of many years of careful planning and living. She walked into her realtor's office full of anticipation. She sat down and accepted Rita's offer of a cup of coffee. She hugged the warm drink with her hands and savored the moment—and no wonder.

Sofia was ready to sign papers to buy her dream house *with cash*. She was 32 years old, single, and ready to reap the benefits of following a financially strategic path since high school.

The final cost of her house was $194,872, and Sofia still had $1,000 left over after providing a cashier's check for the full amount. She was only ten years out of college and had driven the faster track to own her dream house debt-free.

Author's Note

Sofia is a fictional character, but I have met many real-life Sofia's who have turned their dreams into reality. As I listened to their stories, I was inspired to accelerate the payoff of my own mortgage and to write a book that would motivate and equip others to make their dream house come true.

This book follows Sofia's progression from her early years all the way to financial success. You will meet her uncle, RON, who provides practical advice to help her along the way. Later, we will compare the track that Sofia's friend Connie chose with the one Sofia traveled. Their stories make it clear that many different tracks are in front of each one of us, and the one we choose will impact the course of our entire life.

It's time to learn a mentality and strategy that you can apply to your life to realize your debt-free dream. To do this, let's go back sixteen years to join Sofia and Ron as they begin a life-changing conversation.

Family Reunion

Sofia had attended many family reunions. A couple of years before starting college, she experienced one that was very different.

The day they gathered that summer was especially hot. After a picnic feast, her cousins ran off to play the usual sports and games. She didn't feel like getting all sweaty this time, especially with her long blond hair blanketing her neck and back, so she sat in the shade with the adults.

Sofia's Uncle Ron found it difficult to converse with his brother Bill. Ron tried to be interested and engaging, but they didn't seem to have much in common. After an awkward pause in the conversation, Ron turned to engage Sofia in small talk. He asked about her college and career plans. She was happy to share her goal of becoming a nurse. He mentioned that one of his neighbors was a nurse.

When Sofia asked Uncle Ron how he liked his own work, they both lit up. You see, Ron was a realtor, and Sofia dreamed of owning her own home someday. She wondered if he might be willing to share a few tips to help her along toward that dream, not realizing what a goldmine she just discovered. She started firing questions at him as fast as he could answer them.

Sofia wanted to know all the steps of buying a house. And Uncle Ron was thrilled that she was interested in his field of work and was trying to get educated so far in advance. Most of his young clients had no idea what they were getting themselves into when they started looking for their first houses.

Uncle Ron pulled off his NASCAR ball cap to scratch his head. Then he shared one of his favorite analogies.

> RON: If we approach this process as a car race, there are basically three questions you need to answer.
>
> - Do you want to enter the race?
> - If so, do you want to be on the fast track?
> - Or, would you rather be on the faster track?

Sofia was a dry sponge wanting to soak up whatever wisdom he was willing to share.

Enter the Race? To Buy or Not to Buy

> RON: The first question is whether you really want to own a house.
>
> SOFIA: Why do you ask?
>
> RON: There's great pleasure in owning a house, but with it comes great responsibility. Here are a few things to consider regarding homeownership.

He pulled a NASCAR pen from his pocket and drew two boxes on his napkin. In the first box he wrote "Advantages," and in the second box he wrote "Disadvantages." Then he wrote some key words in each column and proceeded to explain each one.

Advantages	Disadvantages
• **Security:** A house can provide a certain amount of protection, comfort, and familiarity. • **Privacy:** In a house, you have more privacy than you do in an apartment (where the walls can be thin). • **Elbow room:** A house can provide more space, especially to raise a family. • **Equity:** A house builds value over time. • **Expression:** Some people are meant to create, build, or decorate, and a house is an ideal place to do this. • **Hospitality:** You probably won't feel as conspicuous entertaining in your own house as you would in an apartment building.	• **Shackle:** How many people have passed up job opportunities because they couldn't sell their houses? TIP: If you are only going to live someplace for less than two years, renting is generally recommended over taking the risk of buying a place and then not being able to sell it. • **Cost:** It is easy to spend a lot of money on homey extras simply because you own it. • **Maintenance:** You are the landlord. If it's broken, it's your problem.

RON: These are a handful of considerations for you to think about. You will likely come up with more pros and cons once you start thinking this over. This may be more detail than you want. I realize my excitement for this topic normally outpaces my listeners. Just wave the red flag when you've had enough, and there won't be any hard feelings!

SOFIA: Not at all. I'm asking because I want to hear what you have to say.

RON: All right then. The decision really boils down to values. What is important to you? Do you value control, privacy, and equity or do you value flexibility, simplicity, and traveling light?

SOFIA: What's equity?

RON: Good question. Let me think of an example. Okay, let's say you buy a car. When it's worth $30,000 and you still owe $25,000, you have $5,000 of equity in the car. If you sold it, that's how much you would have left over.

SOFIA: That helps.

RON: Now, if you don't own, or decide you don't want to own a house, then we can skip to the faster track for ways to save money on rent. There are dramatic ways to trim your budget in the process of renting so you can save more money for vacationing, college savings, and retirement.

SOFIA: Can we come back to that? I'll probably rent during college, but my real goal is to own a house debt-free as quickly as possible.

RON: Okay, so you think the benefits outweigh the costs of owning a house?

SOFIA: Yes. I know most kids my age don't think about owning a home, but I'm a geek.

Getting on the Track

RON: Then let's get on the track and start saving for a down payment. I'll tell you how you can get your dream house, and have it paid off way before most of your classmates.

SOFIA: My helmet's on, Uncle Ron! Let's go.

RON, *smiling*: Great! Now, what are you willing to give up?

SOFIA: Give up? What do you mean give up?

RON: Most people spend everything they make. You cannot save up for a down payment unless you spend less than you make. Many people think, "If we have anything left over at the end of the month, we'll set that aside for a house." It doesn't work that way because we can always think of more things to spend money on. That's why so many people have more month than money. They don't just spend everything they make—they spend *more* than they make.

If you want to have your dream house, you'll have to intentionally divert some money into savings, and that will require a conscious decision to give up something or some things. So, for example, maybe it's ice cream every night before bed.

SOFIA: What? Who told you?

RON: Maybe it's a media subscription.

SOFIA: Ouch!

RON: Maybe it's giving up some free time to get a second job.

SOFIA: Are you serious?

RON: Yes, it takes a lot of time, work, and money. As we talk, I think you will agree that the investment you make in this process will be well worth it. Then you can have your ice cream (and cake) and movies and free time back. But everything we say "Yes" to requires saying "No" to something else—in every area of life. I'm going to say that again, so you don't miss it. Everything we say "Yes" to in life requires saying "No" to something else.

If this scares you off, go back to the fundamental question: How badly do you want a debt-free dream house?

Sofia was quiet. She hadn't realized there would be such hard choices to make so early in this journey. She had hoped it would just be fun, but her gut told her that Uncle Ron was speaking the truth. She had to process this new information.

SOFIA: Uncle RON, I'm going to go grab a brownie. I have a feeling we'll be talking awhile. What can I get you?

RON: I think I'm okay, Sunshine, but thanks.

Ron figured she would probably find someone else to talk to or join the cousins instead of resuming this conversation-gone-bad. He felt bad for going straight to the hard choices. On the other hand, he liked Sofia and didn't want to mislead her into unrealistic expectations. If this idea of going without some things turned her off to buying a house, better she knew that now. But when she emerged from the house, she came straight toward him and plopped back down in her lawn chair.

SOFIA: Uncle RON, thank you for being honest with me. I realize I don't really know much about this whole process. Would you walk me through it a step at a time?

RON: You're serious, aren't you?

SOFIA: Yes.

RON: Okay. To have extra money you either need to cut expenses or add income—or both—if you want to speed up the process.

Sofia relished this simple, yet valuable, information even as she felt its value sinking in and taking root. She had a hunch this conversation was going to make a profound impact on her life.

RON: Take some time to list all your expenses and see if anything stands out to you. The very act of recording expenses produces a subtle side effect. Maybe there will be some cuts you can make that will be relatively painless, or maybe you'll want to make deeper cuts. Think of a flat tire.

SOFIA: Why?

RON: If you are in a car race and you have a flat tire, you don't worry about scratches in the paint. You fix the tire and get back on the track. In financial terms, start looking for big items that are slowing you down. Look for what is costing you thousands of dollars rather than trying to save pennies by using a little less toothpaste each time you brush your teeth.

Real Life Example

RON: I still remember when your mom and dad decided it was time to buy a house instead of renting. They wrote down everything they spent in an expense ledger.

The logbook became their first stop after coming home every evening. It was a very conscious effort. But because recording every expense was a hassle, they started spending way less money than usual. Within sixteen months they had saved enough for the down payment on their first house.

SOFIA: Is that really true?

RON: You can ask them.

He motioned toward her father who was napping in his lawn chair in the shade of the big maple tree.

SOFIA: I'll take your word for it.

RON: I would recommend setting aside an amount from every paycheck or every month before you pay any other bills. Just make sure you have enough to pay your bills. In order to do this, you may need a budget plan.

SOFIA: I've heard of that many times, but no one has ever really explained it to me. What is a budget plan?

RON: Budgeting is telling your money where to go instead of wondering where it went. In order to set a budget plan, you simply need to add up all the expenses that you normally incur each month and write them down. Then adjust to match your priorities.

If you have never set up a budget plan before or have gotten away from following one, there is a simple worksheet at the back of the book to help you with this (see Appendix 2).

RON: The easy part is to plan where your money will go. The hard part is to follow your own plan.

SOFIA: Especially when ice cream is on sale!

RON: Yes, especially then. Well, on second thought, maybe that's when you buy it.

SOFIA: So, I don't have to stop living?

RON: No, I just want you to take this process seriously. Now, if you add up all your income for a month and subtract all your expenses, what's left over is available to save toward a house. At this point, you may see the need to cut some expenses to free up even more savings.

It's wise to put this money in a separate account, if possible, so it's more difficult to access. It'll be tempting to rob from this surplus fund if you are not in the habit of saving. At first, it'll take a lot of discipline to leave this money alone, but, after a while, it'll get easier and easier. Eventually, your excitement will grow as you accumulate a larger amount.

SOFIA: So how much should I save up? What should be my goal?

RON: I would recommend you save about 10 percent of the cost of the first house, and while it might sound confusing initially, about 25 to 50 percent of the cost of the second house, and maybe a third house. Then, if you follow my advice, you should be able to pay cash for your dream house and still have money in your pocket.

SOFIA: Are you serious? Do you really think this is possible?

RON: Absolutely! I've met hundreds of people at various points along a continuum. Some have paid off their houses at young ages, some never will, and most are somewhere in between. What makes the difference?

He gave her a chance to answer. She shrugged and tilted her head. Her brown eyes said, "I don't know."

RON: It's very simple. I'll share with you the secrets I've learned from those who have paid off their houses early. The people who never will pay off their houses either don't know these secrets or don't want to make the effort to accomplish this feat. But these secrets will work for you and anyone else who applies them to their own situation.

SOFIA: Sounds like shortcuts through a maze. I appreciate you sharing them with me!

RON: Well, I'm excited to! After all, you seem genuinely interested. And you are one of my favorite nieces.

SOFIA: Aww, that's nice.

RON: And the more I talk to you, the less I have to talk to my brother Bill.

They both laughed and looked around to see if anyone might have heard them.

SOFIA: Thank you.

RON: I haven't told you much yet.

SOFIA: I always thought that school was where you got an education. I never thought of getting an education from my family.

RON: Hmm...

SOFIA: Why save different amounts for the first and second house?

RON: First, it will seem to take forever to save up for your first house. Waiting too long could get very discouraging. Second, and probably more importantly, I'll show you how to use your house to build equity. The sooner you can start this process the better.

SOFIA: But why 10 percent? Aren't there programs that only require three or five percent down payments?

RON: Good question. The answer is yes, and I'm recommending you use these programs for your first purchase. But if you only save up three percent for a down payment, then what money will you use to fix up the house? On the other hand, if you save 10 percent and only put three or five percent down, you already have money for surprises and improvements. If you don't need it all, you can always throw extra on the mortgage payment to accelerate the payoff, but chances are you will need this money for something you did not expect.

SOFIA: What do you mean, "throw extra on the mortgage?"

RON: Well, each payment consists of principal and interest. You can pay extra each month, and that extra money will go towards principal, which saves you lots of money over the long term. I can explain that in more detail later.

SOFIA: Okay. Let's pretend I'm out of college. I've decided to buy a house, and I've already started saving for a down payment. What are the steps I need to take before I'm in my own house?

Start Looking

RON: Once you have decided to buy and you are saving up for a down payment, it's time to look around.

SOFIA: But I wouldn't know what to look for.

RON: Exactly! That's why you should start looking around. You will get an education about what is available in the market and in what price range. Unless you have been looking for a while already, this will be a reality check experience. You might be very encouraged, or more likely, you might be very discouraged.

Necessary, Nice, and Not Important

RON: You also will have an opportunity to discover which house features will be most valuable to you, which features would be nice, and which features don't really matter at all. In fact, I would suggest making a separate list for each one of these categories. For example, things you think are necessary, nice, and not important. On your necessary list, you might put lots of storage space, close to downtown, etc. Then there are things that would be nice, like two bathrooms, guest room, not near railroad tracks, etc. Then a list for the things you don't care about: a fenced in yard, fireplace, etc.

Another benefit from looking around is that you will develop a clearer picture of what is out there, as well as what you will have to pay for the kind of house you want.

Oh, and another important thing that will happen as you start looking for a house—you will visualize yourself living there. *Where will I put the couch? Which way will I face the bed?* This can be very empowering for people who have never had the confidence that they could buy a house, let alone a dream house debt-free.

Strangely enough, your goal here is not to find the place where you will live. It is simply to get an education and fuel your dream. It will enable you to clearly identify and confidently bid on the right place when it does come along, as well as to adjust your expectations and plans.

SOFIA: What kind of adjustments?

RON: Maybe you will realize that you are going to have to save up more money. Maybe you will realize that you won't get as nice a place as you had hoped. But that's all right.

SOFIA: Why?

Develop a Pit Stop Mentality

RON: You know how a racecar driver will make temporary stops so the pit crew can refuel, change tires, or make other adjustments for maximum performance back on the track?

SOFIA: Yeah, I guess so.

RON: On the fast track, you stay in the same house and pay it off as quickly as possible. On the faster track, you need to see a house as a temporary pit stop to improve your overall performance.

In other words, don't just see houses as residences, but also see them as tools to help you build equity—to accelerate your progress toward your dream house. This frees you from the fear of making a mistake or from getting stuck in a place you don't really like. This also gives you hope that someday you will live in your dream house with no debt.

I've met people in their sixties who still have thirty-year mortgages.

SOFIA: Really?

RON: Yep. You, on the other hand, could have your dream house completely paid off in eight to twelve years from the time you graduate from college.

SOFIA, *tilting her head with a hint of skepticism mixed with a gleam of hope*: You really think that's possible?

RON: I know it is. I've seen it done by many dedicated people.

So, what I am proposing is not easy, but it is very simple and very freeing. Think like a racecar driver coming in for a temporary pit stop—there temporarily, not to stay. Don't plan to find your dream house right away, and you will save yourself a lot of disappointment. Plan to find a place that helps you now. But don't plan to stay in your first house, and maybe not even in your second house. Make your mistakes with those. Get experience and build equity. Figure out what you want with those houses. Then when you have some serious money built up and you know what you want, go buy it.

SOFIA: A pit stop mentality.

RON: That's right.

SOFIA: I get it. I like it.

Capital Gains Tax

RON: Let me show you an example of how the pit stop mentality will help you really get ahead. If you buy a rental property for $100,000 and sell it several years later for $150,000, you have made $50,000. This is an oversimplification, but this is how the concept works. This extra $50,000 is your capital gain. The good news is that you just made $50,000. The bad news is that your poor Uncle Sam needs some money and wants some of your gain.

SOFIA: But I already pay income taxes!

RON: That's right. But Uncle Sam believes in diversification. So, he collects different kinds of taxes from his rich nieces and nephews. This is separate from income taxes, but you report it and pay it at the same time you're filling out your tax return.

SOFIA, *letting out a heavy sigh of disappointment*: Oh.

RON: Capital gain is currently taxable at 0 percent to 20 percent, depending on your income. This number may change over the next few years, so check current rates when you get there.

Let's say you make enough earned income that you pay 20 percent tax on your $50,000 of capital gain, or $10,000. That cuts into your profits, but you still have $40,000 more than before. That's progress.

SOFIA: I suppose. But capital gain tax slows things down?

Residential Tax Exclusion

RON: Yes. That's how it works for an investment property. Now let's consider how this works with a house that you live in. You buy it for $100,000 and sell it for $150,000. Do you still pay $10,000 capital gain tax?

SOFIA: I don't know.

RON: It depends. If you owned and lived in that house for at least two years before selling it, then you get what's called a residential tax exclusion. In other words, you pay no capital gain tax when you sell the house.

SOFIA: Nice!

RON: Not only that, but you can exercise this exclusion an unlimited number of times during your life.

SOFIA: Whoa!

RON: To summarize, you can buy a house, fix it up, live in it for two years, sell it, make a profit, and pay no capital gain tax! Not only that, but you can turn around and do again over and over. This can really help you build equity fast, but it can be very taxing on a relationship. Sorry for the bad pun, *he chuckled*.

SOFIA, *moaning*: Oh dear.

RON: It's a lot of work to fix up a house and then move. It can be an emotionally draining experience, especially if you have become attached to the place. The more work you do on a house, the more likely you are to become attached. So be willing to move from a starter house to another house to build equity, but also be willing to re-evaluate and adjust your plans as necessary to keep your sanity!

The residential exclusion is a good reason to stay for at least two years, but there is also another reason. It will likely take two years to fix up a place to the point where it is worth much more than you paid for it. I'll explain some of the many ways you can do this but understand that this process takes time.

Now it's my turn to stretch my legs. Can I get you anything while I'm up?

SOFIA: I would love another brownie.

While Ron was gone, Sofia found a piece of paper and pen and starting writing notes to herself. She knew from her experience in school that these ideas would fade from her memory with time. She wanted to capture them while they were still fresh.

Soon Ron returned.

RON: Here's your chocolate fix. And now get ready to meet the lender.

SOFIA: I thought you were a realtor?

RON: I am. I was talking about the next step in the process.

Meet with a Lender

RON: Interview a loan officer at your bank or credit union, or a mortgage broker, until you find someone you are comfortable with. If they treat you like they don't really need your business, they don't. Move on to the next interview.

Interview Questions

SOFIA: I thought bank officers would be interviewing me to see if they could trust me with their money?

RON: They do. But you should interview them too. It's a two-way street.

SOFIA: Do I just stop in or call ahead to make an appointment?

RON: Good question. I would call ahead.

SOFIA: And what questions should I ask?

RON: Some examples might be:

- What is your specialty? (For example, loans for businesses, residential houses or commercial buildings? You obviously want someone who specializes in residential loans.)
- What special loans or programs do you have for people with my circumstances and how do these programs work? There are programs from FHA (Federal Housing Administration), HUD (Housing and Urban Development), VA (Veterans Administration), RD (Rural Development), and so on.
- Why should I work with you instead of someone else?
- If I decide to work with you, will you go through my credit report with me and help me clean up any errors?
- Are you willing to educate me on the loan process before we get started?
- What is your typical cost structure for the entire loan process? Can you itemize the common fees? (These will not be quotes, but estimates.[1])

RON: If the lender treats you with respect and is willing to educate you and shop for you, you have found the right person. It is normal for your mortgage professional to take some time to explain the entire loan process to you. If you have questions, feel free to ask. You are not wasting this person's time. In fact, you are ahead of many people because of your budgeting, saving, and already looking around.

---

[1] See Appendix 3 for a list of the common loan fees and costs.

SOFIA: Why do you suggest meeting with a loan officer before finding a house to buy? That seems out of order.

RON: Sof, you have good questions! By meeting with a loan officer first, you can get "pre-qualified" or "pre-approved" for a loan.

Prequalification

RON: Once the loan officer is confident you can be taken on as a client, you should receive a letter of prequalification. This letter will show how much the institution is willing to lend you. You may or may not need to furnish a copy of this letter, but if you can tell your realtor or seller that you have been pre-qualified, you'll be seen as a serious buyer.

With pre-qualification, you are not yet approved for a loan. But with all the information provided to the loan officer, that person should be able to tell you your credit rating and explain where you fall on the credit scale. It will be wise to go through your credit report carefully. There are inaccuracies most of the time, and some of these can have a negative impact on your credit rating. Again, a good loan officer will be willing to help you interpret your credit report and fix errors. It helps everyone in the process because the cleaner your credit report, the better your loan rate will be, and the easier it will be for the loan officer to get your loan approved.

SOFIA: Okay, what's the next step?

Start Looking—Really!

RON: Now you are ready to find a house. If you find a neighborhood you like, watch for real estate signs in the front yards. Any realtor can show you any property listed with the Multiple

Listing Service. Just call a realtor for an appointment to see the house. You can rarely just show up and walk through unless there is an open house in progress.

SOFIA: What is the Multiple Listing Service?

RON: This is a listing of houses from all the participating realtors in the area.

SOFIA: What about houses for sale by owner?

RON: You may find some real deals this way. Just be aware, you may run into some strange scenarios too.

SOFIA: For instance?

RON: Sellers may have very inflated values for their property. They may or may not know what they are doing. Or they may hope you don't know what you are doing and try to take advantage of you. Most people trying to list properties themselves, however, are do-it-yourself types trying to save some money on the sale of their house by cutting out realtor fees.

Whatever reason they are not using a realtor, you still have no representation. So, unless you are very comfortable navigating the search and sales process alone, I would recommend working with a realtor.

SOFIA: I don't have a clue about all this stuff, so I definitely want a realtor.

RON: As you do your research, take down numbers and call the real estate agents listed. You will be amazed at the different kinds of treatment you will receive. Some agents will follow up quickly and professionally. Some will be slow to return your call, if they ever call back at all. Some will be more flexible and accommodating than others. Some will be gruff, and some will be very friendly.

Once you find a realtor you like, stick with that person. This will reward the one who fits you best and keep things simpler for you.

SOFIA: But what if we want to see a property another realtor has listed?

RON: No problem. Any realtor can show you any property.

SOFIA: What do you mean by that? I figured you call the person on the sign, and they show it to you.

RON: That's common. The realtor listing the property probably knows the property well, but they primarily represent the seller.

SOFIA: Is it bad to have them be the one to show the house?

RON: Some would say so, but I don't see it that way. They are motivated to make everyone happy and make a deal happen because that's how they get paid. I think it's fine to have the listing realtor show you a property.

Now, if you have the same person show you each property, they really get a feel for what you think is necessary, nice, and not important. As they get to know your preferences, they can steer you away from places that would waste your time and toward places that would be a more likely fit for you.

SOFIA: That makes sense.

RON: And the more specifically you describe what you are looking for, the easier it will be for your realtor to find appropriate houses. Let me give you a couple of examples.

Let's say you are a realtor, and someone tells you, "I want a place where I can really feel at home!" or "I want a three bed/two bath house in the Oakridge neighborhood where we can build a lot of equity in two years and resell it." Which of these descriptions would be more helpful to you?

SOFIA: Definitely the second description.

RON: Figuring out exactly what you want will help you and your realtor. Another advantage of having the same realtor showing you around is that a realtor can line up several places for you to see, one after the other, saving you a lot of time.

SOFIA: Uncle RON, you should teach a class on this. You are good at explaining things.

RON: Actually, I do. I teach some of this material at a local community college. It's primarily for people who want to become realtors, but I'm sifting out the boring technical stuff and giving you the gold nuggets.

Tips as You Start Looking

RON: Have you heard the three rules of buying real estate?

SOFIA, *giving him a quizzical look*: No...?

RON: "Location, location, location." For example, find the worst house on the nicest street you can afford. You don't want a rundown house in a rundown neighborhood. You want a house that people drive by and say, "Too bad that one is so dumpy looking. It's a nice neighborhood." Guess what? If you buy that house and fix it up, they will want to buy that very same house from you! Then you will be paid handsomely for all your hard work.

SOFIA: Aah.

RON: Take pictures and notes on each house. You may think you will remember each house in detail, but after four or five different showings, they will start to blur together.

"Was that the one with the funny staircase? No, it was the one with the crayon all over the kid's bedroom wall."

You will be very glad for a handful of strategic photos to help you remember which house is which.

Also jot down things like address, asking price, likes and dislikes, obvious improvement or repair issues, etc.

While the details are fresh in your mind, give each house a grade. You will want to separate the "really like's" from the "maybe so's" from the "definitely not's". For example, give each house an A, B, or C grade.

SOFIA: That's simple.

Going Back

RON: Always, and only, go back a second time to see the houses that interest you. As you narrow down your options to only a few, ask what price the realtor thinks you might get each place for now, and how much you might sell each one for once it's fixed up. It wouldn't hurt to ask for comparables or "comps" to back up these estimates.

SOFIA: What is a comparable?

RON: A realtor can print a report showing what similar houses have sold for recently in the same area. Though not a guarantee, this report is a good way to gauge what a house's selling price is likely to be.

When you go back for a second look, take someone with you who understands buildings. This could be a contractor you plan to hire, a very handy person you know, or a home inspector. You will need to pay an inspector for a full report. Any experienced person will probably agree with the following three "don'ts":

- Don't be dissuaded by cosmetic items that can be easily remedied with mowing, raking, weeding, cleaning, painting rooms, mopping floors, cleaning carpets, replacing a broken window, and picking up trash and limbs.
- Don't under-estimate the big-ticket items. Calculate the cost of these carefully and realistically. Big ticket items include a new roof, septic system, well, windows, electrical service rewiring, major plumbing work, or a kitchen remodel.
- Don't even consider a house with a deal breaker issue:

1. A badly cracked foundation
2. Multiple building code violations: If several problems are in plain sight, just think what might be hiding inside the walls and attic.
3. Evidence of significant mold presence or damage: If this is localized to a small area because of a leak that is repairable, that is different. Significant problems would be an entire basement wall or bedroom ceiling.
4. Significant termite damage: If you can see that many of the floor joists are badly damaged, just think what you can't see.
5. Noticeably uneven floors or roof lines: This is evidence of poor construction and/or materials.

If you can't decide between two good choices, go back a third time and take someone else with you for a fresh perspective. Write out the pros and cons of each place and compare them. A winner should surface through this process. If not, be prepared to make an offer on both places.

SOFIA: You can do that?

RON: Yes.

Make an Offer

RON: Okay, so you have looked at, let's say, 15 different houses and you have picked a winner. Now you are ready to make an offer. This is one of the most exciting and scary steps you will take as you move into home ownership.

SOFIA: How do you know how much to offer? I mean, I don't want to cheat anyone, but I don't want to get ripped off either.

RON: That's easy. I have two words to help keep this part of the process in perspective: **Get help!**

You will be tempted to take this step way too seriously, so let other people help you. Otherwise, you might go to extremes as you just mentioned. You should listen to your realtor first. After compiling market surveys, a realtor can give an objective picture of what the going rate is for the house. He or she will have some background information that would provide additional insight, like knowing about special reasons why the seller is very motivated or special terms he or she might agree to.

Include others as well. Realtors, even very experienced ones, can be surprised. If you can, get someone who has bought and sold several properties to give you a different perspective, along with their reasoning. This may be more subjective, but it will still be helpful. Don't involve too many people, or it will get confusing. Just get someone to affirm your decision or point out a big oversight.

After you have some objective and subjective feedback, you will likely develop a gut feeling for what you should offer. Go with this number and outline your contingencies.

SOFIA: What's a contingency? Like a plan B?

RON: Contingencies are conditions that must be met for the sale to take place. Besides your offer amount, you can condition the sale on:

- Various inspections, like a general building inspection or specific inspections like termites, mold, radon, water test, water damage, windows, heating/ventilation/air conditioning systems.
- Certain repairs, like the seller needs to replace the roof, furnace, carpet, etc., or provide an allowance for these repairs.
- Certain items being included in the purchase, like furniture, appliances, drapes, leftover building materials, etc.
- The seller paying part of the closing costs, although some of these will be yours no matter what.

RON: The more contingencies you include, the more insulation you have created. This is good and bad. It protects you from loss, but it may keep the seller from accepting your offer.

SOFIA: For example?

RON: Let's say you are the seller and there are two offers on the table for similar amounts of money. One is a buy "as is" type offer. The other asks for several contingencies. Which one will you accept?

SOFIA: I see what you mean.

RON: Look for a balance between protecting yourself from bad surprises and making your offer attractive to the seller.

Make a Deposit

RON: When you make an offer, you also will need to provide a deposit, which demonstrates that you are a serious buyer.

SOFIA: How much does this cost?

RON: Usually somewhere between a few hundred dollars and a few thousand dollars. But the good news is, this isn't an additional cost. Either you will end up buying the house and your deposit will count toward the purchase, or you won't reach an agreement and you'll get your deposit back. If an agreement is reached, this money goes into an escrow account and is accounted for at the closing.[2]

SOFIA: I see.

RON: Once the realtor collects your deposit and puts together a written offer, including any contingencies, you will sign it. Your realtor will then send it to the seller's realtor to present to the

---

[2] An escrow account is a temporary holding account. See Appendix 3 for a more in-depth definition.

seller. They will have an amount of time that is outlined in the offer to respond to you. This will seem like a long time, whether it is a few hours or a few days.

They will either accept the offer as submitted or, more likely, send you a counteroffer. They may want some of the contingencies removed or more money than you have offered. They will outline these changes from the terms you have laid out and send the offer back for your approval.

This process can go back and forth several times using the technology of the day. Each time you counter-offer, you initial the changes until you both agree on the terms of the sale.

At that point, you both need to sign the contract in its final form. Then you will both be legally obligated to fulfill your side of the agreement. In fact, if you back out of a signed purchase agreement, you will forfeit your deposit. The seller is legally entitled to this money.

Revisit the Lender

RON: All right, once you get a signed offer on a specific house, you can start the official loan process. Your lender will already have most of the needed information on file but may need some updated or additional information.

Getting a loan approved is a process. You will not usually meet with a lender and have an approved loan by the end of the meeting. The lender may be able to pre-qualify you that quickly, but there are more steps to approving your final loan. If you want a preliminary meeting to find your ideal loan officer, just set an appointment and meet him or her.

Once you are ready to start the loan process, you will need to bring additional information for the purpose of credit and financial history. Each institution will have its own requirements, so ask your loan officer for a list. The following are examples of what you may be requested to furnish: pay stubs, tax returns, statements from your bank or investments accounts, social security number, etc.

SOFIA: What about I.D. theft. Is it okay to give out all this information?

RON: You may feel vulnerable sharing this private information with someone you hardly know, so make sure you deal with a reputable firm. Understand, though, that it is normal to release this information during the process. If you are uncomfortable, have someone with more experience join you. They can reassure you or caution you based on the circumstances.

Before the application is completed, a closing is normally scheduled for a certain time and place. The goal is to complete the loan process and have everything ready on time for the closing. The realtor will likely keep tabs on this process also, as he or she does not get paid until the closing. Once your application is complete, your loan officer will send your information to an underwriter who will review everything to determine if you are a good credit risk.

Your credit rating will determine your interest rate. In other words, the lower the risk of lending you money based on your credit and financial history, the lower your interest rate. And the higher your income and savings, the more money the institution will be willing to lend you.

SOFIA: How long does the company need to decide?

RON: For the entire process, including checking for a clear title, etc., one month is a normal turnaround time. Don't panic if you don't hear anything within a week or two. Some situations require even more time. You may have to wait longer, even if you are prequalified, but check with your loan officer every couple weeks to see if steady progress is being made.

Right then, Sofia's mother, Marcia, came up and put her hand on Sofia's shoulder.

Marcia: You two sure have been talking a long time.

RON: You have quite a daughter, Sis. I've always liked her, but I never realized how sharp she is.

SOFIA: We've been having a great talk about buying houses.

Marcia: That's nice. But we need to leave soon, so I wanted to give you a five-minute warning.

RON and SOFIA, *together:* Okay.

Close on the House

RON: Are you ready to leave, or do you want to buy the house before you go?

SOFIA: You know I want to buy my dream home!

RON: Just making sure. A closing is when you sign paperwork to transfer the property from the seller to the buyer. This is usually conducted by a title company, though it can be handled by the lender, by an attorney, or by a realtor, and often takes place at whatever firm is conducting the closing. Both the buyer and seller will commonly be there along with both realtors.

SOFIA: What do I bring to the closing?

RON: You do plan ahead, don't you? You usually bring a cashier's check from your bank for a predetermined amount, your driver's license and not much else. The title company has already searched the official records to make sure there is no lien on the property. This is important because you don't want someone showing up with a prior claim or unpaid bill down the road that you must resolve.

SOFIA: What happens at the closing?

RON: First, you will feel like you are signing your life away because there will be a large stack of papers to sign. Most of these are directly related to the mortgage, but there also will be things like waivers, disclosures, and a closing summary. This is all normal, and someday it will all be electronic.

Logistically, every closing will look different. But at the end of the transactions, the seller gets paid, the realtors get paid, and you get the keys to the house.

SOFIA: And who pays the realtor commission?

RON: The seller usually pays for the real estate commission because the buyer normally empties his or her pockets to cover the down payment. The seller, on the other hand, receives money at the closing, so it is quite practical for that person to pay for the real estate commissions.[3]

SOFIA: Would I then own my own house?

RON: Legally, yes, and practically no. Your lender can put a lien against the property in case you don't repay your loan. In that sense, until you pay it off completely, the lender still has fingers on it.

Well, kiddo, I have really enjoyed talking to you, but I see your parents are slowly making their way toward the car, so I think they really might be leaving. If you're still interested, at next year's reunion I can tell you how to get on the fast track so you can pay off your house in twelve to fifteen years. Then you can remove the lender's fingers completely from your dream house and be the owner.

SOFIA, *giving him a big hug*: Uncle RON, thank you for all this information, and next year you can expect me to take you up on your fast track offer!

---

[3] See Appendix 4 for an explanation of how real estate commission is calculated.

PART 2—THE FAST TRACK

Dream House Debt-Free in
Twelve to Fifteen years

When the next summer reunion came around, Sofia could hardly wait to pick up where she and Uncle Ron had left off. Finishing at the potluck line, she made her way over to him. After a bear hug, she started in.

SOFIA: Do you mind if I grab this seat? After all, we have a date at the races, don't we?

RON: You remembered!

SOFIA: You bet I do! You said you would teach me how to get around the fast track and pay off my house in twelve to fifteen years.

RON, *smiling*: I did. The nice thing about the fast track is that you don't need to be a rocket scientist or brain surgeon to follow it. All you really need is determination and discipline.

SOFIA, *with a twinkle in her eye:* So, even I might have a chance?

RON: I didn't mean that. I just mean that it is simple. It's not easy, but it is simple.

There are very few people who will tell you to pay off your house early, especially if we are in a low-interest-rate environment. There are even fewer who will tell you *how* to do it. In fact, there are people who will tell you *not* to pay off the house for specific reasons.

SOFIA: Oh, really?

RON: Yes. First, I will tell you *why* I think you should pay off your house early, using a simple acronym. Then I will explain why some people will try to talk you out of doing this, but it's important to really think through their arguments—what I call Math versus Myth. Then, if you are interested, I'll show you *how* to pay off your house early.

SOFIA: Sounds good to me.

RON: Why pay off your house early? I use the acronym, **G.E.T. C.A.S.H.**

This acronym contains a mix of objective and subjective points to consider.

G ood Investment: Unlike a mutual fund, you can sleep in your house. Unlike an annuity, you can entertain friends in your house. Does it normally produce income like other investments? No. Can it? Yes. Is it a financial liability while you are paying it off? Yes. Is it a store of value? Yes. Do houses normally appreciate over time? Yes. So, is it a traditional investment? No. Does it have some of the positive qualities of an investment? Yes.

E motional Relief: I have met scores of people who have paid off their houses. **None** I have talked to has ever regretted it. On the contrary, they felt a huge sigh of relief and a feeling of freedom as soon as they paid off their house. You can't put a price tag on that.

T ax Advantages**:** Do you remember when I explained the capital gain exclusion last year?

SOFIA: *slowly shaking her head*: No. Sorry.

RON: If you sell your house after you have lived in it for at least two years, you receive a tax exclusion on any gain. In other words, Uncle Sam wants you to fix up houses and move. It's good for neighborhoods and the economy. Not only that, but the more you have improved and paid down the house by the time you sell it, the more equity you keep—tax-free.

C ash Flow: What would your budget feel like if your mortgage was gone? Wouldn't that be like getting a sudden, large pay raise?

SOFIA: My ice cream budget just went up!

RON: Nice.

A void Interest**:** Every house payment includes interest. But once the house is paid off, you don't pay any more interest on it. Will you still have taxes, insurance, and utilities to pay? Yes, but no interest. And the quicker you pay off the mortgage, the more interest you can save.

S ave for Future: As soon as you pay off the mortgage, put some of that extra money into a savings and/or investment account, where it can grow for future use. Someone came up with this saying, "Those who understand compound interest, receive it...those who do not, pay it."

SOFIA: But don't most people pay interest?

RON: Yes, they do. So, be the one who receives interest as often as possible. The last letter is H.

H ave Options: Without a mortgage, some people could work fewer hours, change jobs, or even retire. How would you like that kind of freedom?

SOFIA: I would like that a lot! **G.E.T. C.A.S.H.** I'm not sure I understand all of it, but I like it.

Math versus Myth

RON: Then let me go into a little more detail. Not just so you understand, but also to honestly explain how not everyone would agree with me. Over the years, I've spoken with many people who wanted to pay off their houses. Some even had the money to do so and a vague sense that it would be a good move, but one thing consistently held them back. Their instinct told them "yes," but their accountant or investment advisor or a friend said "no" for different reasons. There seems to be a lot of traditional advice that is based more on myth than math.

However, is the traditional advice based on common practice or common sense? How many times is the caution against paying off the house backed up by hard numbers?

SOFIA: I don't know.

RON: I had to find out for myself, and what I found was surprising. Not only can someone get ahead by paying off the house, but depending on the circumstances, they can get *way* ahead.

SOFIA: I'm still with you.

RON: Maybe you've heard about the young husband who came into the kitchen and saw his new bride fixing a special meal. She was in the process of cutting off the end of a roast, and he asked, "Why are you doing that?"

"I don't know," his wife replied, "but that's what my mother always does."

The young husband suggested, "Let's call your mom."

Upon receiving the call, her mother said, "I don't know why, but that's what my mother always does."

They called grandma, and she said, "I cut off the end of my roasts, so they'll fit in my pan."

Ron and Sofia both laughed.

SOFIA: That's funny, but what does it have to do with paying off a mortgage?

RON: Although it might be easier to follow common practice than common sense, it's always good to ask questions!

SOFIA: I have a question.

RON: What's that?

SOFIA: Do you need more brownies like I do? I'll get you some while I'm up.

RON: Sure.

SOFIA: Do you want anything to drink while I'm at it?

RON: Yes, but I'll get the drinks, and you get the chocolate.

SOFIA: I'm in for Aunt Pat's famous pink lemonade!

Once they both returned, Ron continued.

RON: Let's take a closer look at the reasons that are given for not paying off the house. Are they like cutting off the end of the roast because someone else does, or does this make good sense?

By the time we're done, you can speak intelligently and confidently on this subject. More importantly, you will save yourself and your friends thousands of dollars—even tens or hundreds of thousands of dollars—by applying these principles.

SOFIA: I'm all for that.

Myth 1

RON: It's easy to think that the house just costs the purchase price. That's true if you pay cash for it. But if you borrow to pay for it, you must pay for the use of the money.

SOFIA: Pay for the money?

RON: Let me explain. When you want to see what the engine of a car looks like, you "pop the hood." Let's pop the hood on a mortgage and see how a mortgage payment is built.

What if you don't have enough cash to buy a house outright—which most people don't? You need to *buy* some money or at least the use of it. When you buy the use of money in order to purchase a house, it is called a mortgage. You usually pay back the mortgage in monthly payments, and this normally happens over a period lasting from ten to thirty years. Part of each loan payment represents giving back some of the borrowed money (principal), and part represents the cost of using the money (interest).

At the beginning of the loan repayment period, most of each payment is interest, paying for the use of the money, and a small part is paying back the principal, the borrowed amount.

Ron could see the puzzled look on Sofia's face.

RON: Sof, wait just a second.

Ron went to his car and brought a briefcase back. After rummaging through it, he pulled out some papers.

RON: Here's an illustration so you can see what I'm describing. This example involves a thirty-year mortgage on $150,000 at 7 percent interest. Look at the first two lines on this page.

Monthly Payments	Beginning Balance	Principal	Interest	Total Payment
1	$150,000.00	$122.95	$875.00	$997.95
2	$149,877.05	$123.67	$874.28	$997.95

RON: This payment of $997.95 repays only $122.95 of the original loan amount the first month. The other $875.00 goes toward interest.

SOFIA: What?

RON: That's right. If you fast-forward to the end of the thirty-year term, it's the other way around. The total payment amount has not changed, but the amount that goes toward the interest has decreased significantly, and the principal amount has likewise increased.

Ron turned a few more pages.

RON: See the following summary of the entire last year:

Monthly Payments	Beginning Balance	Principal	Interest	Total Payment
349-360	$11,533.43	$11,533.43	$441.97	$11,975.40

RON: You'll notice that the **whole last year**, months 349 through 360, there was only $441.97 in interest. The amount of principal repaid each year increases, and the amount of interest each year decreases.

SOFIA: Why is it structured this way?

RON: Good question. Multiply $997.95 by 12 months and multiply that number by 30 years. How much would you end up paying for the house? $160,000, $170,000, maybe $180,000?

He paused for effect. Sofia shrugged.

RON: Would you believe **$359,362!?!**

SOFIA: Do you mean the bank gets $359,000 for a loan of $150,000?

RON: That's right.

SOFIA: So, the person who sells the house gets $150,000 and the bank gets over $200,000?

RON: That's exactly right.

SOFIA: No, that's not right! It can't be. They're just trying to make money!

RON: Well, yes, banks are in business to make money—just like any other kind of business. And selling money is profitable.

Here's why I believe they structure mortgages the way they do-with most of the interest paid in the first half of the repayment period. If you sell the house or refinance the loan, the bank has already received much of the interest it is going to receive. This is particularly important because very few mortgages will run their full cycle. Also, the more interest you pay early, the less risk the bank is taking if you should happen to stop paying sometime later.

What really matters here is that paying off a house—on schedule—costs consumers tens or hundreds of thousands of dollars more than they need to spend.

SOFIA: Now I get it. It's not just about being done with payments, it's about saving big time!

RON: Yes.

SOFIA: But doesn't the bank lose out if you pay off the mortgage early?

RON: Like I said, the interest portion of each payment is heavily loaded in the early years of the mortgage, so most of the money the bank is going to make, they make during this time. In fact, if you pay off the mortgage early, the bank wins in two ways. One, they can re-loan this same money and start over. And two, their bigger risk is you not paying off the loan. If you pay it off early, you may have reduced their profit some, but you have completely eliminated their risk.

RON: So, to correct Myth 1, unless you pay cash for your house, you are paying way more than the purchase price.

SOFIA: Got it.

Myth 2

RON: I remember talking to Tom and Terri Taxem. They wanted to know why their accountant was discouraging them from paying cash for their house.

They were selling their condominium for about $250,000 and downsizing to a repossessed house for $130,000. They would have enough money, after paying off their mortgage on the condominium, to pay cash for their new house. No more mortgage!

SOFIA: That would be exciting!

RON: Well, they were excited, until they spoke with their accountant, who told them to keep the cash and take out a new mortgage on the new house.

SOFIA: Why?

RON: He told them they could continue to deduct the mortgage interest on their tax return each year.

SOFIA: Wouldn't that be helpful?

RON: Not necessarily. First of all, their accountant didn't know that Tom and Terri wanted to travel while they were physically able. They were both retired, and Terri didn't want a mortgage if Tom were to die before she did. So, they didn't really want a mortgage and wondered if they were overlooking something. That's when they called me.

I showed them that for every $12 they spent on their mortgage they would save about $1 on their taxes.

SOFIA: Is that good?

RON: The math is that tax deductions rarely save you money, because they usually cost more than they save.

SOFIA: What did Tom and Terri do?

RON: Their mortgage payments were going to be $865 per month, or about $10,400 per year.

I asked them how much they were going to need for travel expenses. They said about $10,000 per year, and I told them they just found it! If they paid cash for their new house, the $865 per month they would *not* be sending to the bank could be used to send them on trips!

SOFIA: That's really cool, Uncle Ron!

Myth 3

RON: Another couple I met, Ivan and Isabelle Investor, had inherited enough money to pay off their mortgage. And they wanted to, but their investment advisor told them, "Over time, the market will always outperform other kinds of investments."

SOFIA: What was he suggesting?

RON: What he was basically saying was that if they kept their mortgage, and kept their money invested, they would be farther ahead in the long run.

SOFIA: How so?

RON: Well, the logic goes something like this: If you are making 9 percent in the market and paying only 6 percent on your mortgage, you are 3 percent ahead by keeping your money invested.

SOFIA: Oh, I see. That makes sense.

RON: You might be further ahead following this plan. Then again, you might not.

SOFIA: Why not?

RON: During the 1990s, the stock market averaged around a 15 percent per year return. This is one of the best decades in stock market history. Then 2000 to 2010 is called "the lost decade," because the return in the market for that time period was basically zero.

He pulled out another chart from his briefcase.

You see, the market goes through cycles. When it's going up for an extended time, we call it a bull market. When it's going down for an extended time, we call it a bear market.

SOFIA: So that's what those terms mean.

RON: What if you invest the money in the market instead of paying off the mortgage, and the market goes down dramatically? You will lose part of your investment until the market rebounds, and you will also lose the compounding growth on that investment amount forever. You are also still paying tens of thousands of dollars in interest for the house.

SOFIA: Oh yeah. So, you should not do this, right?

RON: Am I trying to say you will always lose money in the market? Absolutely not! Each year, the market is more likely to go up than down, and it tends to outperform most other asset classes over time. So, if you are young and optimistic and have most of your extra money in a retirement plan then you should probably leave the funds invested. But the market is unpredictable, so here's my rule of thumb: the more conservative you are, and the less money you have to invest, and the closer you are to retirement, and the smaller your remaining mortgage balance, and the higher the interest rate, the more seriously you should consider paying off the house early.

At the end of the day, most people feel so great paying off their house, that they would do it even if it *cost* several thousand dollars. It's more of an emotional decision. So, my super simple summary is really the **G.E.T. C.A.S.H.** acronym.

Myth 4

SOFIA: Uncle RON, someone told me that my parents shouldn't have paid off our house before I applied for financial aid.

RON: That was my next myth. And what is the math on this? Well, it depends on which college you choose. The equity in a house, the amount you actually own, is not reported on the Free Application for Federal Student Aid, or FAFSA. So, it won't hurt you if your parents pay off the house if this is the only financial aid application you need.

However, some colleges also require a college student to fill out a CSS/Financial Aid PROFILE®. In this case, home equity information is required and will be considered in the financial aid process. Depending on which college you choose, it may work against you to have the family house paid off.

Also, if you are paying off a house early, you need to be careful where the money comes from. If you are paying off the mortgage with a savings account at the bank or inheritance money, this can work very well. However, if you want to liquidate all or part of a retirement plan to pay off the house, there may be serious tax consequences.

SOFIA: Why?

RON: Retirement money is fully taxable upon withdrawal, so taking out a large amount might greatly increase your tax liability. Not only that, but if you are under 59 ½ years old, you may also pay a tax penalty for taking money out of the retirement account early.

As a rule of thumb, using money that has already been taxed is much more efficient than using money that has never been taxed.

I'm a big fan of paying off the house, but be careful about where the money comes from and how it might impact financial aid, taxes, etc.

SOFIA: Uncle RON, you are kind of losing me with all these details. I'm already sold on paying my house off as early as possible. My concern is how to do that.

Payoff Strategies

RON: I'm sorry. I really get into this stuff. Okay, a couple of basics to cover. For all these examples, we'll assume a $150,000 loan at 7 percent interest for a 30-year term.

SOFIA: Got it.

RON: Secondly, everything you pay on your mortgage beyond the required payment, or before it is due, accelerates the payoff process and automatically cuts the interest amount that would be due.

SOFIA: They'll let you do that?

RON: Good question. Not always, so you would need to check with the bank to make sure. But it is commonly allowed.

SOFIA: Check.

Strategy 1

RON: Most of the strategies I'll show you require extra payments. But what if you are really strapped for cash? This first strategy should still be easy to do. Often, there is more than a month from the time you close on your house to the time you are scheduled to make your first mortgage payment. If you make one **extra** payment of $997.95 during this time, you will knock seven months off your mortgage. In other words, you will save $6,894 of interest and the mortgage will end seven months early.

SOFIA: You're not pulling my leg, are you?

Strategy 2

RON: Not at all. Here's another. You can pay half of your mortgage amount every two weeks. Let's say your payment is $997.95 per month. That would add up to $11,975.40 per year. But if you pay half of that every two weeks, or $498.98, the result is one extra payment per year, or $12,973.48 per year.

SOFIA: How does that work?

RON: You make one half payment every other week, for 52 weeks. This would give you 26 half payments—which equals 13 full payments over the course of the year versus the standard 12 monthly payments.

SOFIA: Oh, I see. What kind of difference does that make?

RON: This strategy will save over $50,000 in interest and pay off your mortgage in under 24 years instead of 30 years.

SOFIA: Seriously?

RON: Yes.

SOFIA: Why doesn't anyone teach this stuff?

Strategy 3

RON: Those first two strategies will speed things up without much extra cost. But if you are financially able, you could also make an extra payment every month your first year of the mortgage. Each extra payment your first year saves about six months of payments at the end. In other words, twelve extra payments at the beginning of the loan eliminate about six years of payments at the end of the loan. This could work if two people are both working, but one plans to stop within a year or two of beginning the mortgage.

SOFIA: What if you can't afford to make double payments your first year, or if you're single?

Strategy 4

RON: Then you might want to consider another strategy. Let's say you wanted to cut your loan time in half, from 30 years to 15, would it cost you twice as much per month?

SOFIA: I would think so.

RON: If you pay $997.95 per month for 30 years, you only need to add $350.29 to this amount to cut the loan down to 15 years.

SOFIA: What? No way!

RON: That's the way it works. You can either apply for a thirty-year loan and pay as if it were a fifteen-year loan or you could apply for a 15-year loan and make regular payments.

SOFIA: Why wouldn't you just take out a fifteen-year loan then?

RON: You could, but if you apply for a thirty-year loan, and can't make the fifteen-year payment, you only have to make the lower thirty-year payment. It gives you some breathing room when finances are tight.

SOFIA: Nice.

Strategy 5

RON: Here's another strategy. Let's say you withhold too much in taxes and you get back $3,600 when you file your tax return. Or let's say you get a $3,600 bonus at the end of the year. What if you take your $3,600 each year and pay it on the mortgage? What would happen? You would save about $108,000 in interest and shorten the mortgage to sixteen years and ten months. And that's if you only apply this one strategy. If you combine this with other strategies, you can pay it off even faster.

SOFIA: That's awesome. Uncle RON, these tips are incredible, but you haven't hit twelve years yet.

Strategy 6

RON: Okay, let's say you really want to pay this thing off in twelve years. Combine strategy four and five. You take out a fifteen-year loan or add $350.29 per month to your thirty-year loan and make the tax return/bonus type payments once a year for $2,400, starting seven months into the loan. Your loan will be paid off in twelve years.

SOFIA: Nice. What about the $3,600 number you used earlier?

RON: That would bring your loan down to ten years and ten months.

SOFIA: Wow!

RON: Not only would you be out of house debt that much sooner, but you would save $116,580 compared to a regular thirty-year loan.

The good news is that it doesn't cost you anything extra, in the long run, to use any of these strategies.

SOFIA: I thought you said these were extra payments?

RON: Yes, but all the extra payments are going toward your original loan amount, the principal, which you had to pay back eventually anyway.

SOFIA: Got it. You pay back the same amount of principal either way.

RON: To sum it up, you can buy your dream house and pay it off in twelve to fifteen years, or less, by using your own combination of early and extra payments.

SOFIA: Thanks for sharing all these ideas with me.

RON: You're most welcome. Sof, you're kind of a go-getter. I'm wondering if you might be interested in getting on the faster track, and paying off your dream house in eight to twelve years instead of twelve to fifteen?

SOFIA: Absolutely!

RON: Either way you go, once you are done paying off the house, you have no more payments. It's just like getting a big raise.

SOFIA, *smiling with pleasure*: Then it's back to ice cream every night!

Marcia, *approaching*: Sof, we need to leave soon, but there's someone here I'd like you to meet before we go.

SOFIA, *turning to give Uncle Ron a hug*: Next year?

RON: Next year.

PART 3—THE FASTER TRACK

Dream House Debt-Free in Eight to Twelve years

As her family pulled into the driveway for the next family reunion, Sofia jumped out of the car and ran up to Uncle Ron with a big hug.

SOFIA: I've been looking forward to seeing you all year.

RON: Me too!

It was only as she unburied her face from his chest and pulled away that she noticed the bandage on the side of his face.

SOFIA: What happened?

RON: Oh, it was just a little spot on my skin the doctor wanted to check out. They took it off once, but it kind of came back—probably nothing serious.

SOFIA: Is it cancerous?

RON, *grinning in acknowledgment*: You don't miss much. It could be. My doctor is running some more tests to see what's up.

SOFIA: Will you let me know what they find out?

RON: Yes, Sunshine. I'll let you know.

SOFIA: Okay. Well, I have something for you.

RON: What is that?

SOFIA, *pulling a gift-wrapped box out of her handbag*: I hope you like it.

Ron opened the package with a puzzled look on his face. Pulling back the last layer of tissue paper he saw a checkered flag signed by Jeff Gordon.

RON: How did you know I was a fan of Jeff Gordon?

SOFIA: I asked a little birdy who lives in your house.

Ron looked over at his wife, Jackie, who had a knowing grin on her face.

SOFIA: I told her you have been so helpful to me, and I wanted to get you something you would appreciate. She thought this might be a winner. Well?

RON, *looking in amazement:* I love it!

SOFIA: Uncle RON, I really do appreciate all the time you have spent sharing this information with me. I just wanted you to know that.

RON, *shaking his head in disbelief and fighting back tears*: Thank you, Sunshine.

He gave her another hug.

SOFIA: Sounds like they're calling us to dinner. Can we grab a plate and get on the faster track?

RON: I'm ready.

With plates full, they found lawn chairs where they could resume their multi-year conversation.

An Accelerator Mentality

RON: In every car, there is a brake and a what?

SOFIA: An accelerator.

RON: And what does the accelerator do?

SOFIA: Makes the car speed up.

RON: Exactly. There are accelerators for all kinds of things—not just cars. If you want to pay off your house in record time, just use a combination of the accelerators I will show you, and you will be surprised how quickly you can get ahead.

SOFIA: Pedal to the metal!

RON, *smiling at her enthusiasm*: The first one might surprise you because we have spent so much time talking about how to buy and pay off a house.

SOFIA: Okay?

RON: The rent accelerator.

SOFIA: What?

RON: That's right. Remember the pit stop mentality? Well, there are several situations where renting might be one of the pit stops and it might get you further ahead than buying a house. For example:

- What if you need to move soon or often?
- What if you live in an area where renting is the only realistic option, or much cheaper than buying?
- What if you are not inclined to put extra money into an apartment because you don't own it but know you would spend frivolously on your own house?
- What if you work many hours and don't want to spend the extra time required to maintain a house?
- What if real estate values are dropping in your area and you don't want to lose equity?
- What if most of your social life revolves around someplace besides your residence?

RON: These might all be good reasons to rent—at least until your circumstances change.

But your house-buying friends might think you are wasting an opportunity to build equity if you are "only renting."

SOFIA: What would you say to that?

RON: Well, my house-buying-type friend, my answer would be to build equity without buying a house.

SOFIA: And how do you do that?

The Economics Professor

RON: Whether you are planning to rent the rest of your life, and even more so if you are planning to buy a house eventually, think in terms of building equity. Let me tell you who I learned this from.

Several years ago, I met a retired economics professor and his wife who never had children. They lived in a very plain apartment all their married life and were millionaires. Renting didn't seem to slow them down much financially.

SOFIA: Not feeding kids probably helped some too.

RON: Good point. Most people need to rent while they are saving up for a house. Why not make the most of this opportunity?

SOFIA: I still don't know what you mean.

RON: If you receive flak for renting, you can show your friends and neighbors how their mortgages work and discuss some of the following tips you are using to build equity while renting. Here are some classic ways to squeeze more dollars out of your rental situation:

- Sub-let the apartment, house or condo—this will cut your rent down dramatically.

SOFIA: What is sub-letting?

RON: Sharing. That's when your name is on the lease, but you rent out some of your space to someone else. They pay rent to you, which reduces your out of pocket cost.

SOFIA: What a great idea!

RON: A couple of cautions though: Consider whether you will get along with other tenants and establish house rules before getting locked into a long-term commitment. You also need to make sure your lease allows sub-letting to other tenants.

SOFIA: Note to self.

RON: Here are some other suggestions:

- Share the cost of utilities and other costs with tenants who share your apartment. If you forget to discuss this detail when you bring in a new tenant, it will be hard to convince them later that they should help with these costs. If you have a lease with the landlord, you are responsible for the terms of that lease. If you can solicit help from others, that is to your benefit.
- Share the cost of food with tenants who share your apartment or those nearby. What if you offer to shop for others or cook meals (or both) for a nominal cost? Aren't you both winning? You both need to eat anyway. Why not get paid to do the shopping and cooking?

SOFIA: I love shopping, and cooking...and eating, for that matter! I never thought of getting paid to do them.

RON: There you go.

- Offer to do some work as full or partial payment for the rent. This could be for the landlord or for other tenants. Examples might include:
    - babysitting, pet care, plant care
    - cooking, cleaning, laundry
    - interior decorating
    - yard work
    - fix-it projects
    - collecting rent from other tenants
    - big projects, like roofing, external painting, etc.

- If you live near mass transportation you may not need a car. This can be a huge savings by itself.

SOFIA: Just a minute, Uncle Ron. I need to get one of your fancy notepad napkins and write these ideas down. They're great.

Sofia got up to grab a napkin. Returning with a napkin, a brownie, and a guilty smile on her face…

SOFIA: What? They were right next to each other!

RON, *humored*: I think someone is addicted to brownies.

They both smiled.

RON: Here are some other suggestions:

- Find a place a little off the beaten path. If you are willing to travel a little farther, you might find a better deal than you would downtown—though I would never recommend sacrificing safety for savings.
- Stay long term. The longer you stay, the more valuable you become to the owner by offering less risk and cost to "replace" you. Therefore, some landlords offer a price incentive for signing a longer lease, or they leave the price of rent steady for high quality, existing renters even if they need to raise the rent on other units. They don't want good renters to look elsewhere, though this may not be an issue in high-demand neighborhoods.
- Ask your landlord for a discount because you will do the following:
    - Extend your lease.
    - Move in by a certain date.
    - Make room for a new tenant by moving to a less desirable unit.
    - Pay on time every month.
    - Pay electronically.
    - Pay ahead, one month to one year.

    - Improve rather than abuse the apartment.
- Cut costs on utilities:
    - Turn down the thermostat when not home.
    - Get an apartment that is sandwiched between others, vertically and horizontally. The more thermal cushion you have, the less heating/cooling you will need, which is the single biggest utility expense.
    - Turn off lights when not using them. An exception to this is to turn on lights and/or a radio for an extra security measure if you're in a neighborhood where burglary might be an issue.
- Use on-site facilities like a pool, weight room or laundry facilities rather than going elsewhere and paying extra for these amenities.
- Laundry: If you have multiple people in your apartment and you are renting for several years, it might pay to buy a used washer and dryer versus using coin operated machines. However, if you live alone or plan to stay a short time, this will probably not make sense.
- Furnish and decorate frugally:
    - Use garage sales, classified ads, auctions, thrift shops, etc.
    - Shop clearance specials, especially for next year's holiday items.
- Place whatever you can save each month you are renting into a savings or investment account.

SOFIA: Wow, I never thought of these things. I see how this could really accelerate your progress.

RON: 'Atta girl. Here's another accelerator.

Income Accelerator

RON: Another way to build equity is to increase your income, which provides more money to set aside. Two primary ways to do this would involve 1) increasing income from your primary job or 2) increasing income from other sources.

SOFIA: How can I control what I make at work—doesn't that depend on my boss?

RON: Not entirely. There are many ways to increase pay in most workplaces.

- Work harder. A great deal of time is wasted in the workplace. Which workers do you think will get the most generous raises? Which are most likely to get promotions? Those who seem lazy or ambitious?

SOFIA: Good point.

RON:

- Accept overtime if available.
- Cover holiday shifts, especially if the pay has a higher multiple. You can often make time-and-a-half, double time or even triple time by working holidays. I just wouldn't make this a lifetime habit. You miss out too much.
- Get a degree, certification, designation, etc., that will raise your value to the company, especially if this results in an automatic raise.
- How about this? Do some research to see if you are being underpaid, and if so, simply ask for more money to keep doing what you are already doing.
- A similar idea: Ask what you need to do to get a promotion. Listen and follow through on the answer to this question.

SOFIA: That **is** simple.

RON:

- Get a second job. Many people get second jobs just for survival. If you make enough to support yourself on your primary job, consider getting a part-time second job just for setting aside some extra money.

- Change jobs. Are you in a dead-end situation? Take the steps necessary to get a better position at the same company or move into a completely new field with more potential growth.
- Start your own company. This is not for everyone and is very risky. But maybe you are one of those people who could run a very successful company. One way to minimize the risk is to start a company in your spare time and build it slowly. Once the income is close to surpassing your regular job, make the switch, putting all your effort into your new company.

RON: And what about increasing income apart from a job?

- Ask your landlord for referral commissions if you provide names of good tenants. The additional bonus is that you have more control over who your neighbors are.
- I already mentioned sub-letting. What if you rent an entire house and sub-lease the extra bedrooms to other tenants? If this is permitted, you might even collect enough from the other tenants to cover the entire rent. That means you virtually stay free.

SOFIA: And what if one of them doesn't pay?

RON: Great question. You need to be firm on collecting rent, and maybe evict someone who is mooching off everyone else for rent or chores. It must be a win-win situation.

- To save on room and board for their college-age kids, sometimes parents buy a second house in the college town and provide free housing for their college-age student through roommates' rent.

SOFIA: What about scrapbooking, window washing, or doing yard work for other people?

RON: You're getting it. The list of options is as big as your imagination.

- Barter rent or partial rent for some professional service your landlord needs, like accounting, construction or handiwork, photography, caregiving for a family member, etc.
- Buy stuff at garage sales or auctions and resell it.

Price Accelerator

RON: Let's say you've done some of these things and saved up some money to buy a house. Let's move from renting to buying a house. First, we have the price accelerator. Two people can buy similar houses on the same street in the same month yet pay much different amounts for their two houses.

SOFIA: How could that happen?

RON: Let's say the first person finds a house that needs some work. The second person finds a house that is ready to move into. The first person finds a motivated seller. The second is a motivated buyer.

SOFIA: I see.

RON: One seller is firm on her price; another is very flexible on his price. Why the difference? Their circumstances are very different from each other. If you look for the kind of seller who is flexible on price you will likely get a much better deal.

SOFIA: How can you tell whether a seller is flexible or not?

RON, *reaching into his briefcase, he hands her a paper*: Here is a chart from my class.

Here are the kinds of people that tend to be:

Firm	Flexible
• not sure if they really want to sell at all • strong emotional attachment to property (because they raised a family there, made major improvements, built it themselves, etc.) • not in a big hurry • not much equity built up	• convinced they want to sell • no emotional ties (short stay, inherited house they never lived in, etc.) • need to sell as soon as possible because of circumstances (lost job, relocation, divorce, etc.) • small balance on loan, or none

RON: In other words, some people's main goal is to get as much out of the house as possible. For others, their main goal is just to get out of the house.

SOFIA: I like that.

RON: Realtors will often know some background information that will tell what kind of seller you are dealing with. But sometimes you can tell the difference even if you have never met the sellers.

SOFIA: How would I know if I never hear the seller's story?

RON: The listing might help. Some clues in a listing that someone will be flexible on the price are words like, "desperate, motivated, already moved, must sell, all offers considered, bring all offers…." Clues that someone will not be very flexible would be words like, "price firm, make an appointment, only serious buyers…."

SOFIA: Nice.

Negotiation Tip

RON: Let me throw this in here. What is the simplest way to negotiate?

SOFIA: No clue.

RON: I like to follow two rules of thumb: the "minimum" rule and the "see you later" rule.

SOFIA: You mean "see you later" like, "so long loser, see you later"?

RON: No, let me explain. First, let's consider the "minimum rule." If you ever have a chance to speak with the seller, simply ask, "What is your best price?" or "What do you absolutely need to get out of the property when you sell?"

It's not unusual for people to tell you the truth about their financial situation. If you offer that price, you have a win-win situation. They are not getting less than they need, and you are not paying more than you need. You are using the minimum rule.

SOFIA: That sounds very simple. Does it really work that well?

RON: Not always, but you would be surprised how often it does.

I would recommend this if you are asking for no other favors—no contingencies on the sale. If you are not talking to the sellers directly, but working through a realtor, the same idea stands. Share this idea with your realtor to use in conversation with the seller's realtor. The seller's realtor must be careful what they share, but maybe they can find a number that is almost assured to get a "yes" from the seller because they know the situation. This is more likely when the property has been on the market for a while.

SOFIA: I like it.

RON: Second, let's consider the "see you later" rule. Some would advise you to offer way below the sellers' asking amount, in case the seller is desperate. If you can find out what it is, I would recommend offering just above their bottom-line number.

SOFIA: Why above?

RON: Several reasons. Why be greedy and go below their asking amount? They are not likely to take you seriously, or they are likely to feel that you are taking advantage of them.

SOFIA: I know I would feel that way.

RON: Also, you want to feel good about the price and about how you treated the seller. When you see them in the store a few months later, will you want to avoid them because in your gut you know you took advantage of their situation? Or will you both be glad to see each other? That's the "see you later" rule. If you keep both rules in mind you are more likely to find a win-win price.

SOFIA: Sold.

Down Payment Accelerator

RON: Okay, back to the faster track.

SOFIA: Before we continue, do you want a brownie?

RON: No, but I do need a pit stop.

SOFIA: Let's pull over for a couple minutes and then get back on the faster track.

RON: You got it.

The Meaning of "Loan to Value"

RON: Do you know what LTV is?

SOFIA: Loan to Value.

RON: I'm impressed.

SOFIA: I generally understand what you are saying while we are talking, but during the last two years I've forgotten some of it, so

I've been reading some articles on my own time to keep things fresh.

RON: Great. What difference does LTV make?

SOFIA: No clue. I just remember the term.

RON: If you buy a house that is worth $250,000 and put $50,000 down, you only need to borrow $200,000 or 80 percent of the cost. In this case, your loan to value ratio is 80 percent. If you put down $125,000, or 50 percent, your loan to value ratio is 50 percent. It is that simple. It is not that easy, but it is that simple.

SOFIA: What difference does it make?

RON: The lower your LTV, the lower your mortgage interest rate. And you usually avoid PMI.

SOFIA: What's that?

RON: Private Mortgage Insurance. It's coverage that **you** pay for that protects the **bank** if you stop making payments on your loan.

SOFIA: If the bank is protected, why don't they pay for the coverage?

RON: Their business is to make money. Remember? If they make PMI conditional to getting a loan, the customer doesn't really have a choice.

SOFIA: That stinks.

RON: The good news is, below an LTV of 80 percent you don't have to get PMI. You only need it if you are borrowing 80 percent or more.

SOFIA: So, a bigger down payment can save you money?

RON: In many ways. It's also important to note that if you borrow more than 90 percent through an FHA loan, the PMI never goes away like it eventually does with other loans. Make sure your loan agent explains exactly how PMI works.

SOFIA: What's FHA?

RON: Federal Housing Administration. They provide mortgage insurance on loans made by FHA-approved lenders. In other words, the government is backing the loan.

Rate Accelerator

RON: You know how you can pull your credit score every year for free?

SOFIA: Not really.

RON: Well, you can. But how many people do this?

SOFIA: I have no idea. Why does it matter?

RON: It may not be necessary on a regular basis, but it can be crucial when preparing to buy a house.

SOFIA: Why?

RON: Credit ratings affect interest rates. It would not be unusual for someone with a poor credit rating to pay 1 to 2 percent more for a loan than her squeaky-clean counterpart.

SOFIA: Okay then. But what can you do if you have lousy credit?

RON: Often a loan officer can coach you on how to clean up little things that bring your score down—things like too many cards, overdue small balances, etc.

SOFIA: It sounds like you want to clean it up before you go to buy?

RON: Exactly.

Equity Accelerator

RON: You knew what LTV was. What about equity?

SOFIA: Is that how much you have paid off on your mortgage?

RON: That is a factor. But you can add equity in more ways than just paying off the loan.

SOFIA: Like how?

RON: Let's say equity is how much the house is worth minus the loan. For example, if you buy a house for $200,000 and pay off $50,000, including the down payment and mortgage payments, you have $50,000 equity in the house. The more you put down on the house and the further you are into the mortgage, the more equity you build up.

SOFIA: Okay.

RON: But as I said, there are other ways to dramatically accelerate the buildup of equity.

Bonus Assets Accelerator

RON: Let's say we discover something of value on the property. For example, Fred Finder discovered a bunch of copper pipes the previous owner, Paul Plumber, had left in a shed behind his house. Paul had collected these gradually as they were left over from many jobs over the years. He didn't want the hassle of moving them to his next house now that he was retired.

Or, you'll never guess what kind of trees Wilma Walnut found in a small grove at the back of her two-acre lot. Both owners placed a small ad in the local paper and sold their discovered treasures, which created extra cash to put toward improvements or extra payments on the house.

SOFIA, *in obvious disbelief*: Paul Plumber?

RON: I've changed the names to protect the innocent, but these **are** real examples I've seen.

Extra Property Accelerator

RON: What if you bought extra acreage that you could split into extra lots someday? That could add quite a bit of value to your place. What if there were two houses on the property? You could live in one house and rent or sell the other. What if you have a house built on one of those lots and sold your first house after living there for two years? And you moved into the second house for two years, then sold it? You could sell both houses with no capital gain tax.

SOFIA: Nice.

RON: Your creativity is the only limiting factor here. Here are a few more ways bonus space could help pay for itself:

- Rent out storage space in a spare room or outbuilding.
- Plant a garden and sell fruits and vegetables in the neighborhood.
- Rent out land to a farmer to cut hay or plant crops if you live in the country and own many acres. This is often more than enough to cover the property taxes.

Location Accelerator

RON: A fast-growing area will usually cause property values to increase at faster than normal rates. Between immigration, migration, and population growth, certain areas are always growing even during a recession.

I'm not saying it is always the same parts of the country that grow over time, different communities grow at different times. If you buy a house during a growth spurt, it is likely to grow in value faster than communities that are not experiencing growth. This creates additional equity for the homeowner.

For example, if you buy a house for $200,000 and pay off $50,000—but it grows 20 percent in value or $40,000—the house is now worth $240,000. However, you only owe $150,000, so you now have $90,000 in equity.

SOFIA: Cool!

RON: Or what about being on the edge of town when the new shopping district starts to expand? You may be able to sell your property for commercial use at a premium price.

SOFIA: These ideas must turn many of your real estate clients into repeat customers.

RON: Some, yes, but not as many as you would think because all these ideas involve some risk and time and energy.

Improvements Accelerator

RON: The most common equity kicker comes in the form of making the right improvements at the right time. If you fix up a house as soon as you move in but don't do anything else for 30 years, you won't gain much equity in this process.

At the other extreme, if you are constantly "updating" the house with unnecessary improvements to suit your taste, you will spend a lot more money in this process than you realize, and it won't build as much equity as you might expect either.

That is not to say updates are bad. They can be good, but be honest with yourself about why you are painting that room again. The truth is some improvements add value, but many do not. And for resale purposes, the best time to make the upgrades is right before you sell.

SOFIA: How do you know what to do and not do?

RON: To answer that question, I've distilled a list of ideas from various sources to come up with a list of do's and don'ts. I would include estimated value increases, but this varies dramatically from one geographical area to another, from one study to another, and from one timeframe to another. These are intended to be generic, timeless-type ideas, not accurate estimates for a particular situation or region.

Ron handed Sofia another sheet of paper.

RON: Here are some tips to consider before you sell.

DO:

- Trim bushes, mow lawn, plant fresh flowers in highly visible areas.
- Clean every room carefully, especially the kitchen and bathrooms.
- Put a fresh coat of paint anywhere that needs it—inside and out.
- Organize and store everything possible.
- Finish off existing spaces like attics and basements to create more useful space.
- Move laundry facilities to main floor, if not already.
- Clean, repair, and refinish floors as necessary.
- Update the kitchen by refinishing or painting cupboards and changing door/drawer hardware.
- Change cupboards and counters only if necessary. Shop prices and match the rest of the house and neighborhood—not way above or below.
- Repair roof as necessary.
- Stage the house with minimal furnishings and decorations, flowers, candles, and fresh coffee, if you have already moved.

DON'T:

- Put in expensive landscape walls, trees, fountains, etc.
- Put up wallpaper or paneling.
- Use exotic colors. Keep it neutral.
- Leave clutter laying around anywhere.
- Build an addition.
- Add another bathroom if it will cost a bedroom.

- Replace floors with expensive options like marble or hardwood.
- Completely redo kitchen unless it adds much more space and function.
- Add new windows, swimming pools, air conditioning, fireplaces, decks, etc. In most areas, these will add more comfort than value and are poor investments.
- Replace the roof unless in poor condition.
- Buy a lot of new furniture to stage the house.

SOFIA: Uncle RON, my head is exploding. I love all your ideas, but this is kind of overwhelming.

RON: I'm glad you said that. Don't try to do everything we have talked about. Just pick and choose the ideas that fit your personality, values, schedule, and interests.

SOFIA: Ahh, immediate pressure relief.

RON: Well, Sunshine, you have drained my well of ideas. Two summers ago, we went through how to decide if you want to buy a house and what it involves. Last summer we talked about getting on the fast track. And this summer we moved over to the faster track. If you follow some of these ideas, I know you can have your dream house paid off in eight to fifteen years, maybe fewer.

SOFIA: I believe you. And I don't know how to repay you.

RON, *pointing to the checkered flag*: You already did. Next year, we'll have to talk about something else—like your career.

SOFIA: Or your NASCAR hobby. I look forward to that very much. Thanks for treating me like an adult and sharing all this information with me.

RON: It's been my pleasure, Sof. You remind me a lot of your mom, and we were always close growing up.

SOFIA: Aww, thanks! I must hug you for that, Uncle Ron!

PART 4—THE FINISH LINE

Why "House" instead of "Home"?

Author's note:

> Part 4 includes bonus material that reveals a second meaning behind the title of the book *Dream House Debt Free.* It also exposes a spiritual dimension of Ron's life that he shares with Sofia, but it is less relevant to the process of buying a house. The author believes this is the most valuable part of the book because living a successful life has more to do with how you spend your days than where you spend your nights. However, if you would prefer to avoid this content, simply skip to Part 5.

As a busy college student Sofia hadn't talked to Uncle Ron in several months, but her mom kept her informed regarding his health concerns and the medical tests that he was having. In November, Sofia's phone rang.

SOFIA: Hi, Uncle RON, how are you doing?

RON: Hey, Sunshine. *He paused.*

SOFIA: Uncle Ron... are you okay?

RON: I've never been better.

SOFIA: So why the long pause?

RON: Yeah, well... do you remember that spot they took off my face?

SOFIA: Yes, Mom told me it was pre-cancerous, and they are doing tests.

RON: Come to find out, I have more spots, inside and outside.

SOFIA: How serious is it? I thought you said you've never been better.

RON: Well, that's true, but I wasn't referring to my health.

SOFIA: I'm confused.

RON: So is my doctor.

Sof, over the last few years, when we've been talking about buying a house, did you happen to notice how seldom I used the word "home?"

SOFIA: Not really.

RON: Well, I rarely use that word unless I'm talking about a homeowner. Can I tell you why?

SOFIA: Uncle RON, you can tell me anything you want.

RON: This is more important and more valuable than everything I've shared with you so far.

SOFIA: Wow, that's really saying something. You have shared some great information with me.

The Camping Trip

RON: About ten years ago I went on a week-long hiking and camping trip. We carried all our gear in backpacks and set up camp each night at a new site. It was a real adventure.

SOFIA: Sounds like it.

RON: It also rained every day of the trip.

SOFIA: Aww, bummer.

RON: It was okay at the beginning of the week. By the end of each day, we were cold and wet, and would set up camp, build a fire, dry out a little, and warm up. However, by the end of the week, when all our clothes were wet, and all our gear was wet, and we were dirty and wet, the adventure was gone.

All I could think about on the last day's hike was—I can't wait to get home where there'll be a warm shower and a dry, soft, clean bed waiting for me.

SOFIA: Sounds miserable.

RON: It was. I was feeling sorry for myself. Then the thought struck me: when I get back to my house, I still won't be home. I won't really be "home" until I'm with the One I was made to be with—my Maker. Then I will be *home* forever. Everywhere I go and stay until then is just a pit stop. It's just temporary.

Sofia, *laughing*: Wait, so you got your pit stop mentality from... God?

RON: Sort of. As I was watching a NASCAR race one day, they showed the driver pulling into the pit for a quick tire change and before you know it, he was back onto the track. It was a temporary stop to improve his long-term outcome. Later, I thought of how we could temporarily move into houses to improve our long-term outcome.

It wasn't until that hike I saw the parallel between our earthly houses and our eternal home. The Bible says, "Our bodies are like tents that we live in here on earth. But when these tents are destroyed, we know that God will give each of us a place to live. These homes will not be buildings that someone has made, but they are in heaven and will last forever" *(1 Corinthians 5:1)*.

So now, when I talk about having a pit stop mentality, it has two meanings. It's about using houses as steppingstones to build equity so we can eventually live in our dream house debt-free. But it's become more than that to me. It's also about the fact that we won't live here forever. Sof, I'm going to leave this body someday, but I believe I will be at *home* with God forever. That's my dream home! That's what He made me for—to live with Him.

SOFIA: Is that why they have you pray for the reunion meal every year, because you're the most religious?

Another Perspective

RON: I'm not religious at all.

SOFIA: What? Wait. You're not?

RON: I'll try to explain. I think of religion as trying to do enough good things that we can earn our way to heaven.

SOFIA: Is that wrong?

RON: The problem is, I don't deserve to go to heaven, no matter how much good I do.

SOFIA: Oh, but I don't think God would keep us from going to heaven—especially people like you and me. We're nice and not out to hurt anyone.

RON: I used to think the same way, but not anymore. I see things very differently than I used to.

SOFIA: How so?

RON: If we could do an appraisal on the planet earth, what do you think it would be worth?

SOFIA: Not sure—probably trillions of dollars!

RON: Agreed. Now, like a house, it has a frame, an energy source, a water system, heating and cooling, air purification, etc.

SOFIA: Hmm. It's funny that as a realtor you would think that way.

RON: I believe God built this delicate, complex planet as a gift-house for us to live in together. I also believe God forms each one of us personally and gives us the gift of life.

SOFIA: You sure have a unique way of looking at things, Uncle RON, but I'm still not sure where you're going with this.

RON: Stick with me. If I wanted to pay God back for a planet to live on and the gift of life, what would I owe Him?

SOFIA: If you look at it that way, you'd owe God big time!

RON: Right. And guess how many days I have lived?

SOFIA: No idea.

RON: So far, 17,953 days.

SOFIA: You are weird. Who figures out this kind of stuff?

RON: Your Aunt Jackie thinks I'm weird too. Anyway, I consider each day another gift from God. What do you suppose each day is worth?

SOFIA: Okay, the tab is getting expensive, huh?

RON: If I wanted to pay God back for all these things the bill would be astronomical. Please understand, these are gifts. He doesn't ask us to pay Him back. I'm just trying to make a point.

SOFIA: Alright.

RON: Now, what if He charged me to go to heaven? What do you think an unending stay in heaven would be worth?

SOFIA: I guess I don't know much about heaven. The idea of sitting on clouds with harps isn't exactly thrilling to me.

RON, *laughing*: I would agree, if that's what heaven was like, but the Bible describes heaven as an eternal home with private living quarters in a city built of gemstones with streets of gold. It speaks of a river of life clear as crystal nourishing the tree of life, a tree with new fruit ripening each month; its leaves bringing healing to the nations. And, "There will be no more death, suffering, crying, or pain" *(John 14:1-4; Revelation 21-22).*

Can you imagine a clean city full of peace and joy and eternal health instead of crime and poverty and racial tension?

SOFIA: Honestly? Not really. But it sounds amazing.

RON: What do you suppose rich and powerful people would pay to stay in a place like that for one night?

SOFIA: The way you are describing it, an awful lot!

RON: What do you think it would cost for a year? For a lifetime? For eternity?

Sofia, *soberly*: Wow. My mind is officially blown.

RON: I'm planning to be there, and I want you to be there with me. Can you see how this is more valuable than owning a certain house?

SOFIA: I guess so. Way more. I never pictured heaven as… a real place. You describe it as a place I would really like to be.

RON: And now that I'm getting close, it seems more real and important to me than ever. That's why I'm telling you this.

You see, I have pancreatic cancer and it has spread.

SOFIA: What are you saying? I don't know much about pancreatic cancer.

RON: I may be *home* before next year's reunion. *He paused.* Are you still there?

SOFIA: Uncle RON, I don't know what to say.

RON: Let me explain where I'm going with all this.

Sofia *sniffling:* Okay.

RON: If God has given me all these gifts, and He is building an even better home for me to live in forever, what would you estimate the cost of these things to be? I'm not saying God invoices us for His gifts to us because He doesn't—but what if He did?

SOFIA: You could never put a price tag on all those things.

RON: Exactly. The truth is, the only way any of us could experience life, let alone life with God, is if He gives it to us as an enormous, undeserved gift. He doesn't owe me anything, including heaven. He has already given me so much.

SOFIA: That's really incredible! I've never thought about God being so generous.

RON: Isn't He? But this is only part of the picture.

SOFIA: What do you mean?

RON: Sofia, if God is the source of life, and I pull away from Him instead of toward Him, what am I moving toward?

SOFIA: Hmm. Death? *After a pause,* I can't imagine you moving toward death.

RON: Sof, when I was in college, I was drinking quite heavily and had a sexual addiction. I took advantage of a lot of people. Instead of making me happier, the party cycle was making me feel empty and cheap and hollow. As I looked at people further down the same road, I could see their lives were a mess. A guy on my dorm floor died from overdosing on drugs. I didn't know him very well, but it sure sobered me up—briefly. I didn't want to end up like that, but I couldn't stop my bad habits. They just kept getting worse. Then, one of my good friends got killed drunk driving. That knocked the wind out of me.

SOFIA: I'm sorry. I had no idea.

RON: It made no sense. I wanted to experience life, but I was feeling more and more dead—just going through the motions.

SOFIA: I think a lot of people feel that way.

RON: I had a neighbor lady when I was little that loved God deeply and told me about Him. She said God had done so much good for me. But instead of treating God with gratefulness and cooperation, I was avoiding God, taking credit for most of the positives in my life, blaming God for the negatives, living very selfishly, and trying to figure out things on my own. It wasn't working very well. By college, I had pretty much turned my back on Him—like He was my enemy!

SOFIA: Wow. When you put it that way, it makes me want to think more seriously about God.

RON: You see, Sunshine, it's not about being religious. In fact, it's just the opposite. I was trashing the most valuable gift God had given me—my life. I came to a place where I realized I was so far away from God, and so deeply indebted to Him, there was no way I could ever make it right. *He paused.*

SOFIA: Uncle RON, I don't know why you say you're doing well? This sounds pretty hopeless.

RON: When I started to see some of this, that's exactly the way I felt. I wanted to change the direction of my life, but I didn't know how. Then, one day I was talking to my roommate. He talked about God like he knew him personally, like my neighbor lady did. But he wasn't a religious weirdo. He was nice to everyone and seemed content. I wanted to be more like him. So, I started asking him questions. He told me even though we could never make things right with God through our own effort, there was a way.

I was wide open to hear what he had to say. He said Jesus Christ was the way back to God. God's Son can take us back to His Father. Then we can finally be **home** with Him.

SOFIA: Your dream home.

RON: Exactly!

This guy told me Jesus paid my debt when He died on the cross. And by rising from the dead, He proved He was God's Son with the authority to forgive and heal and renew. My roommate believed that Jesus defeated death forever, including the power of death in our lives, meaning that He can give us a clean start and give us a life of freedom and purpose and meaning, helping others instead of self-destructing.

SOFIA: That sounds nice, but if that's true, then why do we still die?

RON: Good question. I was skeptical too. I didn't know much about Jesus, other than the story of His birth at Christmas. So, I started reading the Bible. What I came to realize was that His life was predicted, in great detail, centuries before He was born. He performed miracles and taught people about the arrival of a kingdom of justice that would make everything right. He also claimed to be the Son of God, which is normally a mark of being crazy.

SOFIA: Ya' think?

RON: Just when so many people thought he was going to usher in a new political power, He died of a Roman execution on a cross. It seemed like the story was over. But three days later he rose from the dead. And, by rising from the dead, He demonstrated He was after much more than beating the Romans--He was after death itself. He returned to heaven, but before He left, He promised He would come back to set up His kingdom on earth, to restore all of creation, make everything right, and do away with evil and death forever. That's why we still experience death, because we are still waiting for Him to come back.

SOFIA: Well, obviously you've done a lot of reading, but why do you believe it?

RON: Because of who He was when I read about Him in the Bible—how personal He was. He listened to people and looked at people and touched people and healed people. He seemed to care about every single person He met. I became convinced He wants a relationship with every single person—even me. The more I learned about Him, the more I wanted Him in my life, to be part of His movement of compassion and justice—His kingdom. His claims stand up to historical scrutiny, but it was He Himself who led me to believe.

SOFIA: So, what did you do?

RON: My roommate told me I needed to confess my sins and surrender to the leadership of God in my life.

So, I did. My words and tears gushed out as I admitted all the bad things I had done to people, and how I had treated God. Sof, after that, I felt clean and alive for the first time since I was a little kid. I felt freedom and joy and peace and hope. It has been a great life with Him. He gave me a great wife and work I love. We have gone through some hard times, but He's real and personal, and He is with us and helps us.

Now, I'm not afraid to die. I don't want to leave my family and friends, especially Jackie, but I can't wait to go to my dream home and be with God forever. That's what I want you to be ready for, Sof. That's why I called you today.

SOFIA: Wow! *She paused.* What you're saying makes sense, but to be honest, it's new to me and it's an awful lot to take in. I would love to have the kind of faith you are talking about, but I'll have to think about this.

RON: I understand.

SOFIA: I have Christmas break in a month. Can I come see you then?

RON: I'd love it if you could.

A Few Weeks Later

Sofia's phone rang again, but this time it wasn't her Uncle Ron. It was her Aunt Jackie, and she was crying.

SOFIA: Hello.

JACKIE: Sofia?

SOFIA: Yes?

JACKIE: I just called your mother, but I wanted to tell you personally.

SOFIA: Is it about Uncle Ron?

JACKIE: Yes dear. Um… he's gone. *She paused.* He thought the world of you, and I wanted you to be one of the first to know.

After a period of silence, Sofia, are you still there?

Sofia, *fighting back tears:* Yes. I'm here. I thought he had more time. I was getting ready to come see him next week.

JACKIE: I know. It was too fast. It hasn't really sunk in yet. He seemed so healthy, but his cancer was further along than anyone realized.

SOFIA: I'm so sorry, Aunt Jackie.

JACKIE: Thank you. Sofia, he was very weak the last few days, but he wanted me to give you a message.

SOFIA: Okay?

JACKIE: He said to tell you he wants to see you again and to keep thinking about your conversation with him.

SOFIA: Aunt Jackie. I'm not quite there yet, but I started reading the Bible after the last time he called me, and it is definitely giving me a lot to think about.

JACKIE: I'm glad to hear that. Will you be able to come to the funeral? It will be this Saturday.

SOFIA: Nothing could keep me away.

JACKIE: I have some other calls to make, dear, but I look forward to seeing you then.

SOFIA: Aunt Jackie, thanks for calling. I really appreciate it. And I am so sorry. I will miss Uncle Ron terribly, and I know you will too.

JACKIE: We all will, dear. But he is finally *home.* Thank you.

After she hung up, Sofia cried uncontrollably.

Finishing the Race

On Saturday, Sofia's entire family went to the funeral. When Sofia walked inside, she was not prepared for what she saw. Draped over the casket was the checkered flag she had given her Uncle Ron at the last reunion. She knew he loved racing, and could tell he appreciated her gift, but she couldn't imagine why it was there at his funeral until the minister explained it.

> MINISTER: The last time I visited Ron in the hospital, he had been reading in 2 Timothy and asked me to share this passage with you: "I have fought well. I have **finished the race**...."

Sofia didn't hear much of the rest of the message. She kept thinking about Uncle Ron finishing his last lap and going *home*. The tears ran freely down her cheeks.

After the funeral, there was a graveside service and a meal for family and friends back at Ron and Jackie's church. After almost everyone had left, Jackie pulled Sofia aside.

> JACKIE: Sofia, there is something your Uncle Ron wanted me to give you.

Sofia looked at her with a grateful, mascara-smudged face. Jackie opened a box and folded neatly inside was the checkered flag that had been displayed on the casket during the funeral.

Sofia burst into tears all over again. He couldn't have given her anything more meaningful, more personal, or more inviting. She would treasure it always... and think of *home*.

PART 5—The Race Is On

One Year Later

Sofia grieved deeply after Uncle Ron's passing, but she continued to go through the motions of life until the heaviest sadness lifted.

She made several friends during nursing school, but her closest was probably Connie. They had many things in common besides nursing, like a love for all thing's chocolate, birthday month, romantic comedies, and working at the same hospital.

One thing they did not share was their approach toward money. Sofia thought Connie could use a little more focus and discipline in her spending habits, and Connie thought Sofia was too uptight about money to enjoy life sometimes. They were probably both right. When Sofia tried to share what her uncle had taught her, Connie's guard went up. She told Sofia they should probably just share chocolate and not ideas about how to handle money.

Sofia's Strategy

After graduation, both Sofia and Connie moved into apartments where they each stayed for four years. They both wanted to own a house and were both saving up for a down payment.

It sounds like both young women were on the same financial track, doesn't it? Well, they were not. Let's back up even further and see why.

While renting, Sofia did several things to get ahead, while Connie fell behind. First, Connie bought a brand-new car as soon as she got her first job out of college. Second, she wanted to get a new wardrobe and some things for her apartment, so she accepted a few of the many credit cards being offered to her and racked up a few thousand dollars of additional debt. Where did she now stand financially?

Connie	**Debt**
School loans	$25,000
Car loan	$30,700
Credit card balances	$5,950
Money in savings	$0
Total debt	- $61,650

Sofia, on the other hand, was in the minority of students that graduate from college without debt.

How did she do that?

First, she found part-time and summer jobs throughout high school and college to save toward college expenses. Second, she took dual enrollment classes that gave her credit for high school and college at the same time. This allowed her to graduate from high school with an associate degree. Third, she applied for as many scholarships as she could find each spring. Fourth, she took a year off between high school and her first year of full-time college to work and save. This is how she earned her bachelor's degree three years out of high school with no debt.

After graduating college and finding a job, Sofia found an apartment a few blocks from her workplace so she could walk. Because of this, she decided she could get by a few more years with her same old car. Sofia also shopped mostly at thrift stores for used and new clothing. Since she paid cash, she did not need to rack up credit card debt. She had one credit card but paid it off each month. Where did she stand as she moved from college into her first apartment?

Sofia	**Debt**
School loans	$0
Car loan	$0
Credit card balances	$80
Money in bank	$500
Total debt	$0

Less than a month out of college there was already a big gap between Connie and Sofia financially. As they moved through life that gap widened even though they were both nurses with jobs paying similar amounts. This was not because of their pay, but because of their mentality.

The Sum of Many Small Decisions Equals Huge Gains

In Sofia's first apartment, instead of absorbing the entire cost herself, Sofia was able to sublet space to another tenant, which was allowed by her lease. She asked her friend Connie to share the apartment. They quickly realized that friends do not always make the best apartment mates. Connie moved into a nicer and more expensive apartment. Shortly thereafter Sofia found another tenant who stayed four years. Not only did they get along most of the time, but they became good friends who helped each other out financially. What was the financial impact of this arrangement?

Sofia's Rent	Roommate's Share of Rent	Sofia's Savings
$1,450/month	$725	$725
$17,400/year	$8,700	$8,700
$69,600/four years	$34,800	$34,800

In other words, just by having another tenant share her apartment, Sofia saved $34,800 over four years!

Sofia did a couple of other things that helped her financially. She enjoyed grocery shopping for deals. Her landlord who lived on the main floor did not like shopping at all. He worked full time and managed the apartment building on the side. When he found out that Sofia liked to shop, he offered to pay her 15 percent of the cost of his normal grocery budget in order to keep him stocked with groceries. In other words, since he normally spent $100 per week on groceries, he offered to pay her an extra $15 to shop for him and keep him constantly stocked with certain basics in his refrigerator and pantry (bread, milk, eggs, meat, fresh produce, canned goods, etc.).

Sofia countered the landlord's offer with a win-win proposal. She offered to keep him stocked on $100 per week instead of $115, with the agreement that she got to keep any savings.

How could he refuse? He couldn't. They had a deal. Sofia made a game out of bargain hunting, so she could cut an average of 30 percent off his grocery bill through coupons, store sales and off brands. He stayed within budget, and she made $25 to $35 per week in the process.

When Sofia's landlord told another busy tenant about their arrangement, she offered Sofia the same deal. This tenant, an attorney, was a bit more particular about name brands, but she also spent more. Sofia saved about 20 percent of the $150 per week budget that this woman normally spent. So, she still made $30 per week in the process. What was the result of this arrangement financially?

Sofia's Offer	**Income from Services per week**	**Income from Services for a 50-week year**	**Four-year Income**
Grocery Shopping	$30 x 2 = $60	$3,000	$12,000

Sofia	**Updated Four-year Savings**
Shared Rent	$34,800
Grocery Shopping	$12,000
Total Savings	$46,800

Lastly, Sofia did all the laundry for her roommate and herself in exchange for her roommate paying all the utilities for the apartment. She figured she had to do laundry anyway, and her roommate said she would rather read than do laundry.

The funny thing was that Sofia read a lot while she did laundry. It did require more loads than just doing her own, but she would start several loads at the same time in the community laundry room, then read during the wash cycle and again during the drying cycle. This took only one evening a week. The extra loads and detergent cost her approximately $25 per month. The utilities amounted to about $230 per month. Her half would have been $115 per month. What was the financial impact?

Sofia's Offer	**Monthly savings/cost**	**Annual savings/cost**	**Four-year Savings**
Savings on Utilities	$115	$1,380	$5,520
Extra cost of Laundry	- $25	- $300	- $1,200
Net savings	$90	$1,080	$4,320

Let's add up Sofia's four-year savings using this approach:

Sofia	**Updated Four-year Savings**
Shared rent	$34,800
Grocery shopping	$12,000
Laundry	$4,320
Total savings	$51,120

She also managed to save just over $100 per month from her paychecks. Let's see where Sofia stands at the end of the four years:

Sofia	**Financial Standing**
Total debt	$0
Rent accelerator savings	$51,120
Extra cash into savings	$5,200
Total savings	$56,320

Sofia set aside all this savings and was very well prepared to buy her first house.

Digging Deeper in Debt

Now what happened to Connie over the four years of renting? She faithfully made payments on her school loans, and her balance was down to $16,747. She managed to pay down most of her car loan, but she got the itch to buy a new car. After three years she owed about as much on the loan as the dealer would give her for a trade-in.

The good news: The trade-in covered the balance of the loan. The bad news: She started all over again with a new loan for a slightly higher amount.

Now she owed $33,000 on her new car, and the raises at work did not quite keep up with her expenses. She raised her credit limit a couple of times and charged some living expenses on a regular basis. She owed $15,890 on credit cards and store cards combined. She made some late payments, but she usually caught up within a month or two.

Where did this put her financially?

Connie	**Financial Standing**
School loans	$16,747
Car loan	$33,000
Credit card balances	$15,890
Money in savings	$0
Total debt	- $65,637

You'll notice that Sofia and Connie continue to grow apart financially. Watch this gap widen as they get into their first houses.

Two Big Differences

Sofia and Connie, both age 26, bought similar starter-type houses on the same street in the same month, yet they paid very different amounts. Sofia paid $125,000 and Connie paid $169,000. Why the difference, and what lessons can we learn from their examples?

Sofia's First House

Sofia found out that the sellers had already moved out of town and bought another house. They not only had two mortgage payments, but also the property tax bill was coming due for their old house. They also were hearing from the city that they needed to have someone come to mow the yard.

Only one other person had looked at the house, but no offer was made. They were very motivated to sell—and quickly. They were asking $150,000, and Sofia offered 80 percent of the asking price or $120,000. They were already thinking about reducing the price anyway, and they countered with $125,000. Sofia accepted their offer and saved $25,000.

Sofia also saved the interest that would never have to be paid on this $25,000 savings. This represented a savings of another $31,887.

Sofia	**Price Savings**
Offering 80 percent of asking price	$25,000
Interest savings on price (at 6.5 percent x 30 years)	$31,887
Total savings	$56,887

Connie's First House

Now the house Connie wanted was in nicer condition than Sofia's. The couple had recently made a lot of updates and upgrades in preparation for selling. They would have accepted $150,000 but were hoping to get at least $160,000 for their house. Naturally, they were asking more for their house and were looking for just the right buyer who would appreciate all the improvements.

Connie fell in love with the house and she fit that description perfectly.

The sellers had inflated the asking price 5 percent (to $168,000) to give themselves some room for negotiation. However, Connie didn't really understand real estate negotiation, nor did she ask for any advice. She wanted to make sure they accepted her offer.

Instead of negotiating a lower amount than the asking price, she offered even *more* than the asking price. She made an offer of $169,000. How could they refuse her offer? They couldn't, and they accepted. This was kind of a win-win situation as both parties got what they wanted.

This came at a premium cost to Connie in more ways than one. She paid a higher price for the house, plus interest on this extra cost. Altogether these added up to $19,000 more than the asking price of Sofia's house.

Connie	**Price Premium**
Offering 1.68 percent above asking price	$1,000
Amount above seller's lowest price	$18,000
Interest cost on premium (at *7.25 percent x 30 years)	$23,146
Total cost	$42,146

*The reason for 7.25 percent vs. 6.5 percent interest rate explained below.

The important thing to notice as we carry on is the compounding effect all these little details create.

Three Mortgage Accelerators

Both Sofia and Connie had a down payment for their houses. Sofia was able to put down 35 percent on her house ($43,750), whereas Connie had to borrow 10 percent from her parents to put down on her house ($16,900). A down payment creates leverage in several forms.

First, because Sofia had saved up a down payment, she would never have to pay interest on the money she put down. Her down payment went directly toward the purchase price. This saved $55,800 of additional interest ($43,750 at 6.5 percent x 30 years) if she kept the loan for the full term.

Secondly, Sofia was able to get a better interest rate than Connie. It is not unusual to save ½ percent on the interest rate for having a 75 percent LTV (**loan** amount **to** house **value** ratio) mortgage. Over thirty years, this ½ percent interest rate savings would equal another $9,364 for Sofia (at 6 percent versus 6.5 percent).

Lastly, because Sofia put down such a large down payment, she will avoid PMI (private mortgage insurance; see Appendix 1).

Since PMI is usually only required when borrowing more than 80 percent loan to value ratio, Sofia will not need it. Therefore, she will save about $40 per month or $4,880 over the term of the loan.

Sofia	Down Payment Savings
Down payment interest savings	$55,800
Down payment interest rate savings	$9,515
PMI savings	$4,880
Total down payment savings	$70,195

In other words, Sofia's down payment of $43,750 could save her up to $70,195 if she kept the loan for the entire term.

How did Connie's situation compare?

As mentioned above, Connie borrowed her 10 percent down payment from her parents. They charged her 5 percent interest on this personal loan and gave her ten years to repay it.

This helped her because this loan did not show up on her credit report, and it was at a lower interest rate than she would have had to pay for a second loan through a bank (8.25 percent). Furthermore, she paid less interest because it was a shorter duration than the mortgage itself. However, she still had to pay it back.

The difference between paying the down payment amount of $16,900 at 8.25 percent over 30 years ($28,805) and paying it at 5 percent over 10 years ($4,610) is $24,195. This represents a substantial savings for Connie. However, she will still owe PMI. Granted, the premium might be only $50 per month. But add that up over 10 years, and she will have to pay $6,000 for private mortgage insurance.

Connie	Down Payment Savings
Down payment interest savings	$24,195
Down payment interest rate savings	$0
PMI cost	-$6,000
Total down payment savings	$18,195

Sofia's down payment strategy saved her $70,195, while Connie's fortunate loan terms from PPB (Parent's Personal Bank) saved her $18,195—a $52,000 difference.

Interest Rate Accelerator

Credit rating affects what interest rate a person can get on a loan. Connie had missed paying a few bills on time and had maxed out two of her credit cards. There were also two cards she had canceled that were still shown as active on her credit report. Finally, there were the car and student loans on her record.

Connie went to her bank and asked what the going rate was for a loan on her first house. They quoted her 6.5 percent, "depending" on her credit score, but her credit issues prevented them from giving her that rate. Instead, she would need to pay 7.25 percent. She figured that wouldn't make much difference as it was only 0.75 percent more. She could have received a better rate at another bank, but she didn't really want to take the time to check around.

Sofia, on the other hand, had used her only credit card regularly and paid it off promptly each month. So, she had an excellent payment history as well as a healthy debt-to-income ratio. Her credit score was very high and qualified her for a discounted rate of 6.125 percent. That was at the first place she checked. As you can imagine, she shopped around for an even better rate of 6 percent from another bank.

Let's compare. How would this rate accelerator affect their actual cost over the course of the loans?

Connie	Rate Accelerator
Interest cost at 7.25 percent	$221,432
Interest cost at 6 percent	$176,190
Interest rate **cost**	$45,242

Sofia	Rate Accelerator
Interest cost at 7.25 percent	$118,287
Interest cost at 6 percent	$94,118
Interest rate **savings**	$24,169

In summary, the rate accelerator saved Sofia $24,169 and cost Connie an additional $45,242. The gap keeps growing between their financial futures.

Term Accelerator

Connie set up her mortgage for a standard thirty-year term, and Sofia set up her mortgage for fifteen years. Let's look at the difference this makes in their housing costs

Connie's	Term Accelerator
Cost for 30-year term at 7.25 percent interest rate	$221,432
Cost for 15-year term at 7.25 percent interest rate	$97,824
Term accelerator cost	$123,608

In other words, Connie will pay $123,608 more by paying her house off in thirty years versus fifteen years. However, she will spend $350 less per month using a longer payment schedule, because a longer mortgage provides lower monthly payments. This gives Connie more breathing room with monthly expenses.

Sofia's decision to pay off her house in fifteen years versus thirty years will require more per month (by almost $200), but this reduces the amount of interest and increases the percentage amount of each payment going toward repaying the principal.

The other benefit of a shorter term is that this usually drops the interest rate even further. In this case, Sofia was able to get 5.75 percent rate on her fifteen-year mortgage instead of 6 percent on a thirty-year mortgage.

Sofia	**Term accelerator**
Interest on 30-year mortgage of $81,250 at 7.25 percent	$118,287
Cost for 15-year term at 6 percent interest rate	$42,164
Interest savings for lower term	$76,123
Rate savings for 5.75 percent vs. 6 percent	$1,967
Total term accelerator savings	$78,090

As you will notice, the higher the interest rate the greater the cost of a longer-term loan.

To combine all these accelerators, if Sofia stayed in this house for 15 years, and if she added up all her savings, it would look like this:

Sofia	**Term accelerator**
Interest for 30 years on 80 percent of asking price of $150,000, or $120,000, at 7.25 percent	$174,700
Interest for 15 years on 65 percent of sale price of $125,000, or $81,250, at 5.75 percent	$40,197
Savings for all strategies combined	$134,503

A thirty-year mortgage of $120,000 at 7.25 percent would cost $174,700 in interest. A fifteen-year mortgage of $81,250 at 5.75 percent would cost $40,197. The savings to Sofia would be $134,503. Think of all the things that could be done with that money! In this case, she did not stay in her first house very long, but she still experienced a significant savings.

After moving into her first house, Sofia cleaned up the leaves and branches that the previous owners had not been able to get to before they moved. Then she borrowed some books and magazines from the library about landscaping. After sketching out some designs, she had some friends over for dessert and brainstorming. They had a wonderful time, and she received some great ideas to add to her plan.

Then Sofia took her plan to a local greenhouse to buy the plants. The owner of the greenhouse looked over her design and made a couple of suggestions. She had mixed sunny and shady plants and slow-growing and fast-growing bushes together in the same areas. Her free "consultation" with the greenhouse owner remedied this situation.

Sofia bought the plants after adjusting her plans. Because she bought all the plants at the same place at the same time, she felt comfortable asking for a 15 percent discount. The greenhouse owner was willing to grant her a 10 percent discount, especially since she paid with cash. They both felt good about the sale.

When the project was completed, Sofia not only had improved the value of the house somewhat, but also her sense of ownership and satisfaction was growing.

Sofia then moved to the inside of the house. The walls needed cleaning and painting. With a relatively small investment here, she was able to make the house look much fresher.

Then she considered what to do with the carpet. It looked relatively new, except for some stains and soiled areas in the walkways and near the front door. She tried cleaning it with some spray-on cleaner. This helped a little but didn't get the carpet completely clean. It was not worn out, but she really wanted to be able to enjoy a fresh look and feel.

A friend suggested having a commercial cleaner come in to work on the carpets. This worked out very well. The cleaning crew was professional and quick, leaving the carpet looking like new. This solution cost her a few hundred dollars instead of thousands of dollars to replace the carpets.

Sofia did not do much expensive upgrading on her house since she saw this as a pit stop and planned to move in a few years. She added some closet organizers and had a semi-retired handyman named Herb finish off a recreation room and office in the basement. She kept sprucing it up and making it more useful.

For example, she bought a beautiful wood fireplace mantle at an auction for $100 and had Herb transport it to her house so she could clean it up. Then she had Herb mount it on her living room wall for another $100. A realtor told her later it really added personality to the room.

Sofia's share of the rent payment had been $725 per month. She had received a few raises and used these to prepare for a higher monthly payment. This first house payment was $674.71 per month, but she was prepared to make "extra payments" of $325.29 per month. This rounded her payment up to an even $1,000 and accelerated the equity build-up in her house.

Sofia ran out of inexpensive projects after about two years and decided it was time to sell her first house. Her realtor did a market analysis and figured she could sell the house for around $162,500 based on the current market.

How did this turn out?

Sofia	**Equity**
Actual sale price	$160,000
Closing costs of 8 percent	-$12,800
Mortgage payoff	-$65,757
Total equity	$81,443

Sofia's Second House

What did she do next? Sofia remembered how much it helped to have extra rent in her apartment, so she decided to buy a duplex and live in one half of it. The other half she would rent out to help make her payments.

Sofia would miss having a house all to herself, but she had a plan, and she knew this duplex was a temporary pit stop on her way to her dream house. She knew she needed to build equity, and she figured this might help. She figured correctly.

She found a duplex in a nice, but modest, neighborhood for $140,000. She put $75,000 down on the mortgage and borrowed $65,000. Her new payment was $1,272 per month at 6.5 percent interest for five years, and another $400 per month for taxes, insurance and maintenance. Her renter paid her $900 per month plus utilities. She was used to paying $1,000 per month, and now her share was only $772. So, she decided to put the $228 difference into extra payments on the duplex.

What did this look like?

Sofia	**Cash Flow**
Mortgage at 6.5 percent x five years	-$1272
Taxes, insurance and maintenance	-$400
Rental income	+$900
Extra payment	-$228
Total expenditures	$1,000

Connie's Second House, Her Dream House

Connie stayed in her first home for 15 years. What a great feeling to just move into a clean, finished house! She paid dearly, though, for this good feeling as we discussed earlier.

Since everything was as she liked it when she moved in, you would think there was no need to change anything. However, Connie subscribed to several house magazines and watched TV shows which gave her an endless supply of new ideas.

She loved the house at first, but when the mood wore off or a new idea came along, she would hire someone to change landscaping, flooring, paint, faucets, lights or doors to match whatever was in style at the time. This cost her a great deal more than she anticipated because she remodeled parts of the house many times before reselling it.

If Connie would have added up all the changes over the years, which she never did, she would have found that she spent about $90,000 over the 15 years she owned her house. Some years she spent very little; some years she made large expenditures.

For example, one year she had a deck built, but twelve years later she had it removed and had landscapers put in a patio instead. She remodeled the kitchen completely two different times, and the two bathrooms one and two times respectively.

The interesting thing is that when it came time to sell her house, the value had not improved as much as she expected. She knew other houses in the neighborhood had sold for $275,000 to $290,000. Connie also knew she had made many more improvements over the years than most other homeowners in her neighborhood. So, she unrealistically expected to receive well over $300,000 for her "nicer" home.

However, she received an offer of only $292,000 when the time came. Though she was disappointed, she had found a house she liked even more and was excited to move on. She took the $292,000.

In the first ten years, she paid her parents back for the 10 percent down payment loan. By year fifteen of her mortgage, she had paid back $38,437 of the $152,100 she had borrowed. She had also paid $148,329 in interest. She still owed $113,663 on the mortgage. So how much equity did she have?

Connie	Equity
Actual sale price	$292,000
Closing costs of 8 percent	-$23,360
Mortgage payoff	-$113,663
Total equity	$154,977

This was real progress. Connie had managed to build up $154,977 in equity in her house. She had also paid off her student loans. However, she had built up a higher credit card balance and continued to purchase a new car every two to four years. She also bought one week of a time-share condominium for vacations. She was making regular payments on that and still owed $17,461.

Finally, she found her dream house. She figured it was not very much more than her current house in price—$350,000 versus $292,000—and when it was paid off, she knew it would be worth much more than her current house. It was in a nicer neighborhood and had more expensive everything.

She didn't like the idea of having so much consumer debt, so she decided to use some of the proceeds of her house to pay off her car, time-share, and credit cards. This would give her a "clean slate" and a little more breathing room for the new payments in case they were more than her previous house.

Connie	Equity in first house
Money left over from sale	$154,977
Auto loan	-$42,300
Time-share balance	-$17,461
Credit card balances	-$27,200
Remaining equity	$68,016

Connie was very pleased. She was going to be able to put $60,000 down on her new house. This reduced the amount she needed to borrow but did mean she would have to pay PMI for a while.

So, where does Connie now stand financially?

Connie	Financial Standing
Cash on hand	$8,016
Loan amount on new house	-$290,000
Value of new house	+$350,000
Value of time-shares	+$30,000
Total equity	$98,016

The good news is she does "own" the new house, and the time-share is paid for, both of which she plans to enjoy for a long time. The bad news is she is starting over with a 30-year mortgage. If she stays on schedule, she won't have it paid off until she is 71 years of age.

Sofia's Dream House

Sofia stayed in her first apartment for four years. She was in her first house for two years, then in her duplex four years. She was 32 years old, and only ten years out of college when it happened. She was driving home from work one Friday, troubled about the increased load of paperwork. She still loved taking care of patients but didn't feel like she was able to spend as much time with them as before. To change her scenery and hopefully her mood, she decided to travel home a longer, but nicer, route. Going through her favorite neighborhood a house caught her eye. It was a two-story structure that looked like something out of a fairy tale.

Rita was putting up a "For Sale" sign in the front yard. She had just listed the house the day before. Sofia wasn't planning to buy a house but couldn't resist the temptation to stop and look.

Since the owners were out of town for the weekend, Rita was able to show the place to Sofia immediately. As she toured the house, Sofia tried to stay calm, trying not to get too excited. She could hardly believe the quality and attention to detail in each room.

Sofia called her friend Herb and asked if he could come over and see the house before she left. He happened to be free and came right over. He checked out the major systems of the house as best he could and told her it was an exceptionally well-built house. The listing price for the place was $215,000.

Sofia went home, her mind spinning with questions and ideas:

- How long before the duplex would be paid off?
- How much did she have in her investment account?
- How much would she need to borrow to buy this house?

- Would someone else see it and make an offer before she had the chance?

She looked up her balance on the mortgage on her duplex. The extra payment of $228 per month had cut almost a year off the loan. She only owed $2,560 more. Next, she checked the balance in her investment account. She had put $500 per month into this account for four years, for a total contribution of $24,000. However, it had earned interest and dividends along the way and was now worth $27,604.

She talked to her tenant, Rick, to let him know she might be selling the duplex and moving. What Sofia didn't realize was how much he had been learning from her about money management over the time he had rented from her. He was thinking about buying a duplex and was saving up to do so, but he didn't know how or when to bring up the idea to Sofia. He also didn't really want to move, so this seemed like a perfect time to make her an offer. Now they were both excited.

Sofia called Rita back with a double favor. Could she come over to write up an offer on the house she had just shown her? Could she also recommend someone to handle the closing for the sale of her duplex? Sofia didn't need to list the duplex as she already had a buyer. Rita was happy to do both. She would handle the duplex closing for a flat fee of $1,000.

As she was discussing the sale of the duplex, Rita asked Sofia what she wanted to get out of her house. Sofia mentioned she had paid $140,000 for it just four years earlier. Rita told her she could run some comparables, but she figured the duplex was "probably worth $170,000 give or take." After she did her homework, it was clear she had been very close. The comps showed the duplex was worth about $171,000.

Sofia	Equity
Market value of duplex	$171,000
Closing cost	-$1,000
Mortgage payoff	-$2,560
Duplex equity	$167,350
Investment account balance	+$27,604
Total equity	$195,044

Now Sofia was very excited. She had $167,350 in equity in the duplex. Plus, she had another $27,604 in her investment account. Rita did not expect someone in her early 30's to have this much equity. She realized Sofia could almost pay cash. Financing would obviously be no problem, as she would need to borrow such a small amount.

Sofia talked to Rita some more about the circumstances of the sellers. This was an older couple who had lived in this house for twenty years, and they were looking to downsize to a smaller house now that the kids were gone. They did not want two payments, so even though they had put an offer on another place, the purchase was contingent on selling their current house.

Sofia thought: If they had lived there for twenty years, it was possible they had built up quite a bit of equity. Perhaps this would give them a little wiggle room on the price. And if they had already made an offer on another place, they were emotionally ready to move. Would it be possible to do a cash deal? She offered them 90 percent of the listing price or $193,500 in cash, as soon as she could close the sale with Rick.

Rita knew the sellers had some wiggle room. Even though she wasn't sure they would take this much off the sale price, her job was to present the offer to them. Their job was to decide to accept or counteroffer. She wrote up the offer, and she also called them to explain what had happened.

They told her that they were encouraged but would have to think about it until Monday. That was a very long weekend for Sofia, but Monday morning the realtor told her they had accepted her offer. Now she went from excited to elated!

Sofia cashed out her investment account that week and put the proceeds in the bank. With Rick's credit score and savings, he was able to get financing within three weeks. They were ready to close. The total cost to Sofia for her new house was $194,872. She would be able to buy her house debt-free and still have a few dollars left over.

Where Are We Going?

She was only ten years out of college, and she now lived in her dream house with no mortgage payment. It had taken a lot of work to get there, but she felt great! She had kept this house a secret so she could surprise her friends. They were following her from her old house, not believing this was her new house.

They pulled over and parked as Sofia had. But why? Where were they? Then Connie looked above the garage door and saw a checkered flag. Was that the one Sofia had told her about, the one she gave her Uncle RON, and he gave back? They piled out of their cars still wondering what was going on. No one except Connie understood the significance of the flag. Connie looked at it again, then gave Sofia a quick questioning smile. Sofia smiled back and nodded.

> Sofia *wiping her tears away as she turned back toward the front door:* Everyone come in, dinner should be ready.

EPILOGUE

The year before Sofia bought her dream house, she met a guy at work who also loved chocolate, and he grew to love Sofia even more. They were married and raised a family in her dream house. He was not a natural saver like she had become, but she taught him the principles that she learned from her Uncle RON, and he gradually came to see the wisdom of debt-free living. They made a lot of mistakes along the way but saved inside and outside their retirement plans.

Twenty-six Years Later

By the time Sofia was 58 years old, she and her husband were empty-nesters. They had a substantial amount of money saved up and were thinking about new adventures.

For 35 years Sofia loved her nursing work. But over the years, regulations caused the amount of documentation required on each case to grow, and the time with patients to shrink proportionately. She had made the adjustment from paper to electronic medical records alright. Then a different corporation acquired the hospital, and she acquired a new boss. Her old manager expected everyone to work hard, but they also had a lot of fun and had become a family to each other.

Sofia's new boss, Dora, didn't understand the word "fun." Everything was about numbers, do more in less time with fewer nurses—push, push, push. Well, some of Sofia's best friends had been let go and a couple others were looking for work elsewhere. Sofia dreaded going to work most days. Dora had just fired one of Sofia's best friends, Jeri, and informed Sofia of that fact at the end of her shift.

DORA: You are one of our best nurses and will be taking on some extra responsibilities as a result of Jeri's termination. I'm sure you understand and will be up for the task.

Sofia had several immediate thoughts. First, she was grieving for Jeri, whom she knew really needed the job she had just lost. Second, she was shocked to hear Dora give her a compliment. That was highly unusual. Then she decided it was probably flattery more than a sincere compliment, considering the circumstances. She would need to sort this out before responding to the news.

SOFIA: I'll have to think about this. I'll see you tomorrow.

Now Dora paused. Maybe she had upset Sofia? Oh well, after a good night's sleep, she would be back to her normal productive self, happy to still have a job.

The next morning, when Sofia walked up to the nurse's station, she looked very pleasant, so Dora was sure she had cleared her mind and come to see things clearly.

Sofia walked into Dora's office and handed her an envelope. A flash of dread came over Dora that Sofia might be resigning—but only very briefly. Dora set the envelope aside and asked Sofia what it was.

SOFIA: I want to thank you for this opportunity.

Dora was relieved to know this was probably a thank you note but was also curious.

DORA: What opportunity?

SOFIA: After work yesterday, my husband and I stopped over to see our financial advisor. She helped us calculate how much we needed from our investment accounts each month to cover expenses. We had no idea we were ready to retire two years ago. Thank you for prompting us to go see her with this question in mind.

Sofia was a little smug. But she was genuinely appreciative, and Dora was genuinely stunned. Could this really be happening? How could she lose Sofia? She had been a great employee. The nursing staff was stretched thin and even Dora knew she couldn't push them much further. What was she going to do now? She slumped into her chair contemplating this when Sofia interrupted her thoughts.

SOFIA: Would you like me to clear my station today, or would you like this to be my two weeks' notice?

DORA, *humbly*: If you would be willing to work for two weeks, I would appreciate it.

Frosting on the Cake

Sofia enjoyed her work again during those two weeks! Not only had Dora become much nicer toward her, probably wishing she would change her mind, but her co-workers took turns taking her out to lunch each day to wish her well in retirement.

The last day she brought the checkered flag to work and hung it above her workstation. Everyone thought it was just a clever joke. Her friend Connie understood the significance of this flag. She knew this flag had been a gift to Sofia's Uncle RON, had rested on his casket, and had been re-gifted back to Sofia. She also realized it had become a symbol of Sofia's own faith, that Sofia had hung it over the garage door of her dream house for the first week she lived there, and that Sofia planned to have it draped over her own coffin someday.

The head of human resources pointed out how much paid time off Sofia had accumulated and informed her about the size of her last check. Wow, she hadn't counted on that. What a bonus—literally!

Now, Sofia is tutoring at a nearby school, helping elderly neighbors, and volunteering in her church. She is spending time with her grandchildren and catching last-minute trip deals to exotic places with her husband. She is enjoying a successful retirement. And when retirement is over, she is looking forward to going **home!**

APPENDIX

Appendix 1—Private Mortgage Insurance (PMI)

PMI does not protect the borrower; it protects the lending institution from the buyer defaulting on the loan.

Once you have 20 percent equity in the house, the lender will drop the PMI requirement. However, that is if you notify them. If you don't ask to have this premium discontinued, they will keep charging you for it until the LTV is at 78 percent or until you have 22 percent equity in the house. This usually takes a little over 10 years at 7 percent interest.

Appendix 2—Budget Worksheet

Expenses:

__________ Savings

__________ Donations

__________ Income taxes, if self-employed

Housing:

__________ Mortgage payment or rent

__________ Taxes and Insurance, if not part of mortgage

__________ Utilities

__________ Maintenance

Food:

__________ Groceries

__________ Meals out

Personal Insurance:

__________ Health premium and Out-of-pocket expenses

__________ Life insurance premium

Transportation:

__________ Public transportation and Car services

__________ Auto loans

__________ Fuel

__________ Parking

__________ Insurance

__________ Maintenance

Debt payments:

__________ School loans

__________ Credit cards

__________ Personal loans

Miscellaneous:

__________ Cable/internet/phone

__________ Recreation

__________ Other

__________ **TOTAL Expenses**

Appendix 3—Common Loan Fees and Additional Costs[4]

- **Homeowner's insurance:** When borrowing money to purchase a house, insurance is required. In many cases, this means buying a policy before closing on the house.
- **Title insurance:** This insurance covers you in the unlikely case that the person who sold you the house didn't actually own it free and clear, or if information on the title was false.
- **Appraisal fee:** An appraisal is needed so that a current fair market value for your house can be established for financing purposes.
    - **Escrow:** An escrow account is simply a temporary storage account where money is set aside for a specific purpose. The real estate agent will use an escrow account as a holding account for your deposit. The mortgage company will also use an escrow account to pay your tax and insurance bills by setting aside part of each mortgage payment for that purpose.
- **Application fee or origination fee:** An origination fee is paid to the bank or lender for their services in creating the loan.
- **Points:** A point is 1 percent of the loan. For example, on your $200,000 loan, you might get an 8 percent interest rate. Or if you choose to pay a point (1 percent of the loan, or $2,000), you may get a 7.5 percent interest rate instead.
- **Credit report fees:** In order to secure a loan, the lender will require a verified credit report. You are entitled to one free report per year. Ask if your lender can use this report.

---

[4] Vohwinkle, Jeremy. 2014. *Fees Involved in Buying a Home*, About.com. December 16. Accessed May 22, 2019. http://financialplan.about.com/od/realestatemortgages/a/homebuyingfees.htm

- **Document preparation fees:** The lender or broker will usually have a fee to cover the preparation of the required documents for the loan.
- **Survey fee:** If an existing survey of the land cannot be obtained, a new survey may need to be conducted in order to determine the exact boundaries of the property.
- **Pest or mold inspection:** While not generally required for a brand-new house, the purchase of an older house may require an inspection for pests, such as termites, as well as mold. This requirement can vary by location.
- **Property taxes:** You may need to reimburse some property taxes immediately if the seller has already paid taxes for a time period where you will be the owner. Also, there may be other municipal taxes or fees for sewer or water that need to be paid.
- **State recording fees:** Depending on where you live, there may be a fee required for recording and holding the information regarding the sale.

Appendix 4—The Workings of Real Estate Commission

The commission for the sale of a house is based on the sale price of the house. For example, if the house sells for $150,000 and the commission is 7 percent, then the commission is $10,500.

The realtor who lists the property and the realtor who finds the buyer split the commission unless the same realtor does both. If the realtor works for a broker, that broker receives a share of the commission and the realtor receives a share.

So, when there is a buyer's agent and a seller's agent, each realtor may receive as little as 25 percent of the total commission, or $2,625, on a $150,000 sale. Also, the costs to list the property on the MLS, to advertise, etc., all come out of the commission.

Now divide what is left over by how many hours they spend on showings, paperwork, and phone calls, and you will see that realtors work very hard to earn their commissions. Lastly, consider that they don't get paid unless, and until, the house is sold.

Some people will advise you to ask the broker to reduce his or her commission to save you money. I'm not a big fan of this unless you do frequent sales with that agent. If realtors are good, don't cheat them. This is an unpaid commercial for a group of professionals I believe are sometimes overworked and underappreciated.

DEDICATION

I thank God for the Uncle Ron's in my life:

Uncle David—A hardworking man who invested in so many young people and hosted so many annual reunions on their farm in Gladwin, Michigan. In my imagination, this is where uncle Ron's conversations with Sofia occurred.

Uncle Bob—Who loved to laugh, loved to eat, and loved to give advice.

Uncle Neil—Always asking about my work and family, and as loyal as a golden retriever.

Uncle Vic—He acknowledged me by shaking my hand vigorously and embarrassed me by asking about my girlfriend years before I had one.

Uncle Horace—He spoke volumes with few words, asking a question here, giving a smile and a gift there.

Uncle Gary—A passionate soul with hearty, contagious laughter.

I also thank God for rescuing me from what would have surely been a self-destructive life, and for inviting me into his family through Jesus Christ.

UPCOMING RESOURCES

This book is a cooperative work between

Overflowing resources

FAMILY FOCUSED FINANCIAL

The mission of Overflowing Resources Publishing Company is to equip people to live an overflowing life, and Family Focused Financial helps poeple plan a successful retirement. A shared aim is to help people prepare for their best future.

At the time of publication, *Dream House* is part of a series still being written.

The prequel is about Uncle Ron coaching two neighbors to understand that when kids learn to love their work, they receive many benefits.

The first sequel centers around Sofia sharing what she has learned with a co-worker about how to retire successfully.

Finally, there is another sequel about Aunt Jackie carrying on after Ron is gone. It demonstrates how to bless your family even as you leave this life, through impactful estate planning principles for young and old.

The author would love to hear from you at caanderson@hirep.net

Made in the
USA
Middletown, DE

77101208R00070